Receive and Achieve...Now!

15 Bible Secrets on How to Find Joy, Success & Abundance in Small Business

by

Terry G. Davis, MBA, JD

with

Rev. David L. Morrow

Foreword by William "Clark" Kent

Copyright © 2013
by Terry G. Davis, MBA, JD with Rev. David L. Morrow

Receive And Achieve. . .Now!
15 Bible Secrets on How to Find Joy, Success & Abundance in Small Business
by Terry G. Davis, MBA, JD with Rev. David L. Morrow

Printed in the United States of America

ISBN 9781619046481

All rights reserved solely by the author. The author guarantees all contents are original and do not infringe upon the legal rights of any other person or work. No part of this book may be reproduced in any form without the permission of the author. The views expressed in this book are not necessarily those of the publisher.

Unless otherwise indicated, Bible quotations are taken from The Holy Bible, King James Version (KJV); The American Standard Version (ASV); The Holy Bible, New International Version®, NIV®. Copyright © 1973, 1978, 1984, 2011 by Biblica; The Holy Bible, New King James Version(NKJV). Copyright © 1982 by Thomas Nelson; The Message(MSG). Copyright © 1993, 1994, 1995, 1996, 2000, 2001, 2002 by Eugene H. Peterson; The Holy Bible, New International Reader's Version(NIRV). Copyright © 1996, 1998 by Biblica; and The New Living Translation(NLT). Copyright © 1996, 2004, 2007 by Tyndale House Foundation.

Disclaimer: The information in this book is not intended to be a substitute for legal, accounting, financial, or other professional services.

Cover Design by: Errol Hylton, Typiconica.com

www.xulonpress.com

To: Pastor Chris Erwin

Thank you for being a wonderful servant, pastor and mentor for me and so many others. May God continue to bless you and your family.

Proverbs 3:5,6

Hi Katie Chris & Erin,

Thank You for being a wonderful Pastor and man of God to us many Years.
May God continue to bless you and your family.

Luke
Phil 3:56

Contents

Acknowledgments xiii
Foreword xvii
Preface xxi
PART I. - THE VICTOR'S MINDSET 29
    -Morning Prayer Statement-

Introduction 31
    The Starting Point 44
    The 7 Universal Steps for Success 50
    Become a Breakthrough Thinker 66

PART II. - FINDING YOUR TRUE CALLING
    AND SETTING THE PATH 73
    -Morning Prayer Statement-

1.   VISION 75
    A Sixth Sense 79
    Try This Exercise 81
    Enlarge Your Vision 82
2.   SET GOALS AND MAKE PLANS 86
    No Boundaries 88
    Setting Goals And Plans For Your Business 91

Plannng Is Fundamental...94

PART III. - THE STRENGTH TO MOVE FORWARD...............107
-Morning Prayer Statement-

3. COURAGE 109
   Conquering Fear..111
4. PERSEVERANCE...119
   Perseverance – The Quiet Strength Within.............119
   Attitude Determines Altitude 121
   The Anger Factor..124
   Preparation is the Key 130
5. PASSION..136
   The Fire Within 137
   Energy to Burn 138
   Passion is Contagious...141
   Avoid Passion-Killers...143

PART IV. - DO IT NOW! 147
-Morning Prayer Statement-

6. TAKE ACTION 149
   It's Really Fear 151
   Opportunities for Learning..153
   On the Shoulders of Others 158
   Spotting the Waves of Change.................................159
   Christ and Social Networking 162

PART V. - YOUR SECRET SAUCE: THE FRUIT OF THE SPIRIT *169*

-Morning Prayer Statement-

7. GOOD JUDGMENT 171
   - Garbage In, Garbage Out 172
   - Be a Strategic Thinker 175
   - Count the Cost and Decide 177
8. INTEGRITY 180
   - First Things First 183
   - Sure-Fire Networking Tips 185
   - Pocket Your Elevator Speech 188
   - Find a Mentor 190
   - The Rebekah Principle 192
   - Information Is the New Currency 193
9. SELF-CONFIDENCE 196
   - Encourage Yourself 199
   - Persistence Pays 204
   - Always Remember This 209

PART VI. - BATTLE STATIONS! 215

-Morning Prayer Statement-

10. GOOD HEALTH 217
    - Silent Killers 219
    - Change Or Die 220
    - But What Can I Do? 225

11.	STAY FOCUSED ON YOUR MISSION –
	MANAGE DISTRACTIONS 230
	Distractions in Action 231
	Course Correction..233
	Financial Distractions 234
	Finding Real Help..235
	The Debt and Tax Bug Bit Me, Too..............237
	Terry's Ten-Step Plan to Financial Freedom............241
	The Millionaire Mindset................................244
	Case Study - How We Got Out of Debt and Stayed Out..................................246
12.	PREPARED FOR SPIRITUAL WARFARE 251
	Make Joy Your Weapon of Choice 255
	Worry is a Lack of Faith..............................257
	Beyond Where You Thought You Could Go..............258

PART VII. - WHAT'S REALLY IMPORTANT 263

-Morning Prayer Statement-

13.	EFFECTIVE TIME MANAGEMENT...........................265
	No Time like the Present............................265
	Priorities: How to Set Them 267
14.	BE A GIVER 272
	Giving is Really Receiving..........................275
	Let Your Goodness Show...........................276
	Favor: God's Power Booster 279
	Favor Has Drawing Power 282
	Favor Keeps You Connected......................284

15	HAVE FAITH IN GOD	287
	Faith and Finance	290
	Faith is a Compass	296

About QR Codes		301
About The Authors		307

Dedication

I dedicate this book to my Lord and Risen Savior, Jesus Christ and all those He calls to spread the Good News to all the world.

I also dedicate this book to my loving wife, Melinda, who I thank God every day for blessing me with a lifetime of her presence.

This book is also dedicated to my children Evan and Gavin, their spouses, Carnell and Karia, my parents Verba, Matt and step-mom Barbara, my sister, brothers, entire family, in-laws and many wonderful friends.

I further dedicate this book to the memory of my cousin, Denzil Rankins, who lived his life with great joy, which he loved to spread .

Last, but not least, I dedicate this book to my (our) first to be born grandson due in February 2014.

Acknowledgments

I wish to acknowledge:

My long-time spiritual mentor, co-author, and friend, Pastor David Morrow, his wife, Vickie, and their children.

My friend, Bill "Clark" Kent, who wrote the Foreword for this book, his wife, Sibyl, their children and the super team at BTL Technologies, Inc.

My senior pastor, Chris Hodges at Church of the Highlands, whose vision and inspirational leadership are providing much needed Christ-centered therapy and leadership for our church, our cities, state, nation and the world. May God continue to bless, protect and prosper his special anointing, his family and all those that his hands touches and influences.

My Church of the Highlands Montgomery, Alabama, campus pastor, Chris Erwin, whose heart and enthusiasm for God's people overflows as he pours out encouragement and words of excellence every day of the week. I pray for God's continued blessings and protection for him and his family.

My awesome church family at Church of the Highlands… You Rock!

Senior Pastor, David Jeremiah, of Shadow Mountain Community Church near San Diego, whose ministry and rock solid teachings I have followed for 15 years.

New York Times best-selling author, Marcus Brotherton, whose review of this book provided me confirmation that it, *too* will be a best-seller in spreading the Gospel of Jesus Christ and equipping the saints for warfare in business.

Christian Bible teacher Joyce Meyer, Bishop T. D. Jakes, Pastors Charles Stanley, John Maxwell, Paula White and Joel Osteen, whom I have never met, but whose spiritual teachings have enriched my life immensely.

Paul and Jan Crouch, who made TBN available to me for many years on those sleepless nights at a time when nothing else was on TV that offered the hope of Jesus Christ.

Dr. A. G. Gaston (1892-1996), entrepreneur and philanthropist, who offered me my first job out of law school and showed me that "poverty is an enemy that can be conquered."

Dr. Percy J. Vaughn, former dean of the College of Business at Alabama State University and Dr. Jayne Goodson, former dean of the College of Business at Auburn University, Montgomery where I obtained my BA and MBA, respectively.

My prayer partner Martha Hawkins whose potent prayers, life story and food at her nationally acclaimed restaurant, *"Martha's Place,"* have been a source of nourishment to me (spiritually and physically) for many years.

Max L. Siegel, a brother in Christ, fellow counselor, and fraternity brother whose book "Merging Ministry and Industry" in the music business has been inspirational for me, but is an anchor for Christian music artists who need to stay focused on the True Source of their success.

My longtime office manager, Dorinda Broadnax, whose ministry and gift of administration has kept me organized and on task for many years.

My editor, Julia Wallace, jwallace@falconbroadband.net, and my copy-editor, Debbie Salter, (http://debfreelancer.com) – thank you for your insight and expertise.

My book-coaching mentors John Eggen and Lorna McCloud at Mission Marketing Mentors, Inc. (http://missionmarketing-mentors.com).

To Chandra Thomas and my great team at Xulon Press.

– I thank God for all of your valuable guidance.

Foreword

A Winning Resource for You
By William "Clark" Kent

I love working in business. It's a field that requires me to consistently bring my A-game to the table every single day I go to work. It's my means of providing for my family, my chosen occupation, and the career path closest to my heart. I can honestly say I love what I do.

But business ownership is seldom an easy road for anyone. When I started my company seven years ago, I faced significant challenges trying to get customers and financing. Today the company is growing at an astounding pace and my business is well on track to exceeding my expectations.

Defining success can be a tricky thing in business. Far too many people define success only by their balance sheets. But success in business involves much more than just positive cash flow. I believe the best way to lead is by example. It's very important to me to run my business with sound integrity, to treat my employees (who I call team members) and all my customers in an exemplary fashion, and to be a leader when it comes to community service. I want to do more than run my business – I want to run my business well, with purpose, confidence, and honor. I believe that this is happening today.

I owe my accomplishments in business to hard work, perseverance, and God's grace. Next to my wife, Sibyl, the person who has helped shape who I am, the success I enjoy in my business can be attributed to Terry Davis – an astute businessman, strategist, business coach and attorney that I met several years back.

Simply put, Terry knows what makes a business tick and he has offered me many valuable insights along the way. He helped guide my hand through the early stages of starting the business, solidifying my vision, gathering the necessary components to launch my business and keep it afloat, then finally growing the business and seeing it flourish. Terry has worked with me on business strategies since my retirement from the United States Air Force. Today, my company employs nearly one hundred employees and we operate in ten states. With Terry being an integral part of our strategic planning, we have invested in good people and a solid infrastructure. We are now poised to take this business to the next level and beyond. We will do that by continually serving our customers with excellence.

I can't tell you how valuable it has been to have Terry as an advisor, business coach, and friend. I've taken the insights he's given me and I have become a coach and mentor myself by developing a system to assist my family members and others in setting up successful businesses. I know the spirit of giving that Terry talks about in Chapter 14 has rubbed off on me because I enjoy opportunities to serve, give back to the community, and speak on principles of success in business – hoping to ignite an entrepreneurial spark in the heart and mind of anyone who will listen.

In the book you hold, Terry has taken many of the same principles he shared with me and is now offering them to you. These principles are wise, valuable, tested, and spirit-filled; I'm confident they work because they worked for me. These principles helped me truly define success and then *become* that success by, being prayerful, laying out my vision and then taking action on my present path.

These principles can help you, too. I am confident you will become wiser and more successful if you study the concepts in this book. Whether you're just beginning your business or you've been at it a few years, this book will be a winning resource for you.

I wish you all the best in your business journey!

– William "Clark" Kent, CEO
BTL Technologies Inc.
San Antonio, Texas

###

Preface

Welcome to *Receive and Achieve...Now!* A book and robust small-business resource that's all about learning, taking action and implementing systems to grow your business and enhance your spiritual and personal development. First and foremost, in this book we are putting the Word of God and Jesus Christ back into the equation and conversation for what it takes to build a successful and prosperous business. It's about a closer journey with Him and understanding that He is with you through the ups and downs of running a small business, no matter what those ups and downs may be. In other words, this is about ministry for the marketplace with an individual focus on you, the entrepreneur. This book contains a proven plan and strategies to help guide you, too, starting right now! Many entrepreneurs, most of whom started as small-business owners, have used the secrets found in this book to help grow, prosper, and find tremendous success. They *received* these principles and strategies and *achieved* amazing results.

This book is about transformational servant leadership, character, service and action. An entrepreneur is a transformational servant leader. As such, the lives of others are impacted and changed by the way you, the entrepreneur, lead your life. The 15 chapters in this book outline and discuss the characteristics and strategies an entrepreneur must have to find joy, true success and abundance in a small business. In exercising these characteristics and using the strategies, the entrepreneur can build a profitable business, impact individual lives, be the hands and feet of God and thereby transform the world.

This book is divided in to seven sections. Each section begins with a motivational *prayer statement* which embraces the principles in the chapters that follow. Read each of the *seven prayer statements* before diving into the book to get an a good overview of the book and what you will learn. As time permits, study each *prayer statement* and the supporting scripture references. I recommend reading aloud, one of the prayer statements each morning during the week and again before bedtime. Allow the affirmation of God's Word to inspire, motivate, minister and strengthen you.

The Introduction could be considered a book of sorts unto itself because it covers the spectrum of personal tools every small business owner needs to have the mindset for producing high levels of value for their customers and high levels of revenue for their businesses. It lays the foundation for continuous individual growth and long-term sustainability in business. Whether you are starting a business or are a seasoned businessperson, you will find this book to be an invaluable, uplifting, and life-changing resource because it is based on an invaluable, uplifting, life-changing resource, God's Word. This book is about overcoming four of the biggest challenges to your success which are fear, lack of knowledge, lack of self-confidence and lack of faith.

This book can be read in a few sittings, yet the principles are by no means simplistic. I encourage you to study these principles in depth and reap the benefits of applying them to wherever you are at this time in your life. Keep and use this book as a reference guide and source of encouragement and guidance. Honestly, the principles in this book are most effective when implemented in ninety-day increments over the course of a year. It will be exciting for you to see how your plans come into focus during that year. Moreover, you will be able to measure the extent of how much you accomplish. You will be amazed to see how much God is blessing you and the path that is set before you! Time passes very fast, so don't wait to get started.

To accelerate your learning and record your progress, you obtain a copy of my *Action Guide and Workbook* at www.receive-andachievenow.com or in bookstores. They are available, along with other helpful resources such as free video training. The Action Guide and Workbook will aid you in setting goals, developing a plan for success, implementing your plan, managing your priorities, managing distractions and more. Also at the end of the Introduction is a QR code (black square). Scan it with your Smartphone (you'll need a QR code reader app) and it will take you to my website where you can access video training material, webinars and more. You can also enter the URL just below the QR code on your computer mobile device to access the same information. The convenient thing about this technology and other emerging applications, including online tools like Google Hangouts, YouTube, Twitter and Facebook is I can provide you current and updated material in real time. I can also include live training or test your knowledge (Test? Heaven forbid!) where we can interact and even see each other just as if we are seated in a traditional classroom, essentially for free. All you need is access to the Internet from any computer, or mobile device. If your device is equipped with a camera, your experience can be even richer. So whether you have an ebook reader or paper copy of this book, you have a world of learning resources at your fingertips. The choice of how you study and learn is yours. Cool stuff, huh?

As you read through *Receive and Achieve . . .Now!* you will find it helpful to look up the Bible scripture references that are cited. Use a version of the Bible such as the New International Version (NIV) or the New King James Version (NKJV), if the King James Version is too challenging to understand.[1] Several versions are referenced throughout the book, including the Message version, which I am new to. But for some difficult passages, I found the conversational nature of this translation provided great clarity as to the meaning of the verses where it was referenced. The key to success in comprehending this book is to dive deeply into to God's Word, regardless of the translation and allow the Holy Spirit to guide you.

One of the best ways to truly learn and master the principles in this book is to order a study guide and teach them to others. After all, the real secret of *Receive and Achieve Now!* is not only that you will become spiritually strengthened, battle-ready and prosperous, but you will become a blessing, mentor, and guiding light for many others. You and I are called to make disciples of all nations.[2] In these difficult economic times, making disciples is more important today than it has ever been. There is a calling on your life to make a difference in this world. There are people out there who need what you have to offer, whether it's through running a business, writing a book or giving your testimony. Matthew 5:14 says, *"You are the light of the world. A city that is set on a hill cannot be hidden. ¹⁵ Nor do they light a lamp and put it under a basket, but on a lampstand, and it gives light to all who are in the house.* The time is now to respond to that calling and share your gifts so others will benefit and God will be glorified. For more information on starting a small group visit www.receiveandachievenow.com.

There are "Power Points" at the end of each chapter. They are a summary and quick reference of empowering principles that will accelerate your progress on this journey. Also use them for talking points in your conversation or teaching points when you assist others. Most of the "Power Points" are covered in the proceeding chapter and some are new points that flow with the chapter lesson. Start a small group of two or three people and teach them to others. Your small group could be family members, friends, business partners, church members or others with similar interests. One of the best-kept secrets to success is that when you surround yourself with people who have similar goals and high aspirations, you dramatically increase the probability of your own success as well as that of your group. You will see some amazing results. As the saying goes, *"A rising tide lifts all ships."*

I am already giving thanks to God for the work that you are going to do and success you are going to achieve. I can do that because I know that God is going to bless you immensely through this process. Through His Word, He is going to empower you, enhance your vision and give you the boldness to step out on faith, using the gifts He has planted in you.[3] I'm excited for you because the ways He is going to bless you are in His Book (The Holy Bible). My book is based on His Word. With His Word as your foundation, I am confident the principles in this book will work for you, once you have mastered them!

The content and stories in this book come from me personally, so you'll notice that I write in the first person to maintain one cohesive flow throughout the book. Pastor David Morrow, my co-author is a pastor, friend and spiritual mentor who provided a variety of insights during the course of my writing. I wanted to acknowledge his support as my co-author.

Finally, as I was preparing to move forward with my book, I received confirmation that God's Word holds true and is the same yesterday, today, and tomorrow. Almost every day, I listen to John Maxwell's, A *Minute with Maxwell* video segments. In a recent segment that really resonated for me, the topic was the word "Bible." In this segment, John Maxwell said as a businessperson he fell in love with the Book of Proverbs. He challenged everyone to read a chapter a day – you'll finish it in a month. Proverbs has 31 chapters. In that moment, I was reminded that this was the identical advice my friend and co-author, David Morrow, gave me eighteen years ago when I told him I wanted to learn more about the Bible. I took David's advice and Proverbs has been foundational and transformational for me as an entrepreneur. Because of the everlasting power of

God's Word, I am giving that same advice to you about Proverbs by quoting the words of John Maxwell when he said in that segment: "*I guarantee that if you read one chapter a day, because it is so filled with wisdom and business sense, you will have half a dozen new thoughts, fresh thoughts, good thoughts in the area of business and success that will really help you and take you to another level.*" Start today!

Receive And Achieve. . .Now!

SECRET TOOLS OF A SPIRIT-LED ENTREPRENEUR AND TRANSFORMATIONAL SERVANT LEADER

Vision

Set Goals and Make Plans

Courage

Perseverance

Passion

Take Action

Good Judgment

Integrity

Self-Confidence

Good Health

Stay Focused on the Mission – Manage Distractions

Prepared for Spiritual Warfare

Effective Time Management

Be a Giver

Have faith in God

Your Name Here   Date

PART I.
THE VICTOR'S MINDSET

I will constantly encourage myself in the Lord. I know that how I feel about myself and how I see myself has everything to do with the levels of success I achieve. I am the head and not the tail. I will constantly seek the Lord, worship Him, pray for His favor and wait with expectation to receive it. I am chosen by God to bear fruit. I serve a God of abundance Who wired me to create abundance in service to Him!

Reference:

1 Samuel 30:6

Deuteronomy 28:12-14 (NIV)

Matthew 7:7-8

John 15:16

Philippians 4:13

Matthew 25:14-30

Introduction

Do you believe that God has a purpose for your life and your business? The answer is absolutely He does. In fulfilling that purpose, God has placed in you a vision and a calling to serve and make a difference in the lives of others. That vision includes a desire for success and an abundant life for yourself and your family. He has set you apart and blessed you with gifts and talents to create that abundant life through entrepreneurship, or stated differently, through a business you will start or one in which you are already engaged. This path can be very rewarding, but it is lined with danger and pitfalls.

For a large number of small-business owners, many are struggling and far too many are failing and closing their doors. Did you realize that according to published reports, 40 percent of all those starting a new business will fail in the first year? It's a fact. Research and statistics also show that 80 percent will be out of business within five years, and 95 percent will close their doors within the first ten years. A worse impact which statistics and research don't reveal are the individuals, the marriages and families that are devastated when a small business struggles and ultimately closes its doors.

The downward spiral has to stop. Offering the same stale solutions has not worked. After starting, growing, and advising hundreds of small businesses and small-business owners for more than twenty years, I have seen what works, what has not worked and most importantly, I have seen what is missing. Without question, the one thing that is missing is the one thing that can turn the downward trend of small-business failures on its head in an instant. That is, a teaching of business success principles based on the Gospel of Jesus Christ. Too many entrepreneurs aspire to find success and prosperity in their own strength often based on trendy, shallow slogans, clichés in books, blogs and websites that leave them feeling empty, lost, and even depressed with no place to turn when their efforts fail. This is when Christ shines the most. That is, in the time of your greatest need.

In the next fifteen chapters of this book, you will learn how to become an entrepreneur whose business will buck the downward trend of small-business failures and find joy, success and abundance. This book is about how to abide in Jesus Christ and find your true calling. You will learn that your biggest challenge to success and abundance is having the right mindset and knowing where to turn for complete guidance in your approach to business. The answer can be found in Psalm 36:8-9 which says: "They are abundantly satisfied with the fullness of Your house, and You give them drink from the river of Your pleasures. For with You *is* the fountain of life; In Your light we see light."

You will learn what it means to have a "Victor's Mindset." You will learn not only how to stay in business, but also create the type of life you desire based on the only Source that can truly sustain you through whatever you face on your journey. That source, of course is Jesus Christ. You will learn the importance of having an effective prayer life. You will learn how to shed that wilderness mentality of fear that blocks your success and tap into the many gifts with which God has blessed you. You will learn how to use your imagination and creativity to develop solutions to situations you face. You will learn not only how develop a strategic plan to track your progress in reaching your goals, you will learn how to implement those plans with confidence. This book could easily have been called *"Equipping the Saints* because my purpose and goal is to be used by God do just that. That is to help prepare you so you can overcome the challenges ahead and create abundance that will enable you to influence change the world around you. God's Word in Ephesians 4:12-13 instructs us as believers in Christ on what our purpose in service to Him must be and why:

> *To equip his people for works of service, so that the body of Christ may be built up until we all reach unity in the faith and in the knowledge of the Son of God and become mature, attaining to the whole measure of the fullness of Christ.*

I am confident that as the biblical principles and strategies in this book are taught and more entrepreneurs unashamedly turn to the Gospel, the number of small businesses that survive and prosper will increase beyond anything we could have thought or imagined.

We are a blessed nation founded upon Christian Principles. As we turn back to the principles and promises of God as a nation and as individual small-business owners, we will experience God's favor in a return to the levels of economic prominence we once enjoyed. Jeremiah 29:11 tell us: "For I know the plans I have for you, declares the Lord, plans to prosper you and not to harm you, plans to give you hope and a future."

Business failures occur for a variety of reasons ranging from undercapitalization, to bad location to poor marketing. But one major reason that is rarely discussed, even for seasoned entrepreneurs, is that failure very often occurs because entrepreneurs have not prepared for the battle that is waged <u>within themselves,</u> when adversity, challenges, or obstacles come. It is naïve to think simply because you have a great idea or are good at selling, that millions of customers will immediately come your way. The single most important ingredient to your success in business is you and the attitude or mindset with which you approach entrepreneurship.

Many entrepreneurs get started on the wrong track because all too often, definitions relating to entrepreneurship focus on profit and revenue generation for the entrepreneur. I prefer to place the focus on service and value creation for customers and clients. It is a mistake to abandon that servant-hood attitude that Jesus Christ requires of us, simply because we are talking about business. Entrepreneurs are really transformational servant leaders born to change the world. It is important to start with a sound definition of what an entrepreneur is. That way, the entrepreneur will have a proper perspective for, the long haul, always be relevant to his or her customers, will understand the customer's needs and have fresh ideas to grow their business. An *entrepreneur* is one who serves others in the marketplace through the offering of his or her goods and services that create value for customers and clients. In other words, an entrepreneur is a solution provider or problem solver who fills a need and is compensated for what he or she provides. Your primary focus should not be on the selling, even though you do have to sell and be good at it to make money. Your focus should be on demonstrating to the customer the benefit and value to them in what you are providing. Take note that it's not about you or the products and services you may want to push on customers. It's about serving your customers with integrity and creating sustained value for them that motivates them to want to buy from you. It's about making their lives more convenient, filling a need or solving a problem for them that gives you longevity and keeps you creatively focusing on their needs that leads to both short-term and long-term profitability. Highly successful business owners will tell you when you create value and a great customer experience, people will consistently beat a path to your door and create the wealth you desire, whether that door is surrounded by brick and mortar or it's in cyberspace or "the cloud." Look at the customer experience at Chick-Fil-A. You always find friendly and courteous employees at the drive-thru window and dining in. Other than winning the lottery or being "born into money," entrepreneurship is the single fastest path the average person can embark upon to build wealth and financial independence. As the person who will chart the course, you are the one who must make plans, set goals, see those plans through, and endure the ups and downs that inevitably occur on the road to success. How you end up has everything to do with the path you set. If you are already in business, the sooner you get your focus in the right place, the sooner you find yourself charting a path that attracts the necessary resources, people and customers and higher sales that will grow your business exponentially.

Your success in business will be ultimately determined by three factors:

1) Who you are,
2) What you believe
3) How you think
3) The principles that guide your life and motivate you to act.

That is why the spotlight in this book is focused on you – the person. You must be certain your personal foundation is built on the rock-solid principles of God's Word so you will be prepared for the challenges ahead that can impede the path to success.

Many people fail to understand that when your personal foundation is built on God's principles, the benefits you receive are immeasurable. *That's why I call them secrets.* You will discover in this book that with a solid foundation in place, your success will not be derailed by circumstances, fear, or a previous unpleasant business experience. You will learn what it takes to persevere. Any homebuilder will tell you the most important aspect of building a house is the foundation. So, too, must you build a solid spiritual foundation in order to weather the inevitable storms that can block your path to the success, joy and abundance that God has for you.

The Bible teaches as found in Matthew 7:24–27 (NIV) that if we want a house that will weather the storms, the foundation must be built on solid rock.

> *Therefore everyone who hears these words of mine and puts them into practice is like a wise man who built his house on the rock. The rain came down, the streams rose, and the winds blew and beat against that house; yet it did not fall, because it had its foundation on the rock. But everyone who hears these words of mine and does not put them into practice is like a foolish man who built his house on sand. The rain came down, the streams rose, and the winds blew and beat against that house, and it fell with a great crash.*

Pundits often say the foundation for a successful business begins with a great idea. Wrong! The foundation of a successful business begins with the principles on which your life is built, the ones in which you put your trust. The words of the scripture bear repeating, *"Therefore everyone who hears these words of mine and puts them into practice is like a wise man who built his house on the rock."* It should excite you to know that with God, you've got a plan – a blueprint for construction that will ensure your joy and success if you follow it. You will learn that God's promise to lead you to a land of *"milk and honey"* in business and all facets of your life is real. But you must trust in Him, have courage, and not become distracted by bad information, difficult circumstances, a checkered past or negative influences designed to shake your faith and throw you off course. You are a child of God chosen to bear good fruit. With Christ at the center of your life, nothing can stop you. God's favor and your success are assured.

After studying the principles in this book, you will be more patient because you'll have learned that no one comes equipped with everything he or she needs to go to the top immediately. You'll be at peace knowing that you are a work-in-progress, gaining in knowledge and growing in wisdom which will transform you.[4] You'll have the power to persevere because you've learned that you don't give up or become despondent at the first sign of a challenge or difficult task. Instead, rely on your faith and you'll become creative. You'll learn to use the gifts, skills, and relationships God has blessed you with to overcome obstacles. You will develop an attitude that thrives in the face of adversity. Fear will not stifle your ability to think, step out, and lead when necessary. For many, these things reveal a whole new way of thinking. You will gain peace and joy on your journey to success because you begin to understand the True Source of your strength.

> *I will lift up my eyes to the hills – From whence comes my help? My help comes from the* L*ord,* *Who made heaven and earth. He will not allow your foot to be moved; He who keeps you will not slumber.* (Psalm 121:1–3 NKJV)

The overriding secret to tapping into that never-ending source of strength identified in Psalm 121 is found in Romans 10:9, and says: *that if you confess with your mouth the Lord Jesus and believe in your heart that God has raised Him from the dead, you will be saved.* From there, the sky is the limit. If you follow His precepts, what you can *achieve* is limited only by the walls of your imagination. Philippians 4:13 says, *"I can do all things through Christ which strengthens me."* In Luke 18:27, you find these words: *"Jesus replied, What is impossible with man is possible with God."* Matthew 21:22 says, *"And all things, whatsoever ye shall ask in prayer, believing, ye shall receive."* Choosing to follow Jesus Christ in all your business endeavors is the best decision you will ever make.

This book will prepare you for the warfare of business. The warfare I speak of is not the type that comes from natural business competitors. It is a spiritual warfare fought in your mind. Many people do not believe that spiritual warfare takes place in the minds of each of us every day. They are unaware there is a constant battle for our thoughts from influences that can put us blindly on a course of certain defeat.

In order to effectively fight the battle of spiritual warfare being waged against you, and claim victory, you must become aware that the forces working against you actually do exist. These forces are fear, depression, addiction, timidity, guilt, shame, anxiety, indecision, and low self-esteem. These are tools of Satan and there is nothing more he would rather have you believe than to believe there is nothing you can do about these forces being waged against you. These forces can derail your plans, shake your confidence and cause you to really be down on yourself. They affect your relationships, your marriage, your productivity, your health, your outlook and your spiritual well-being. Effectively combating these forces begins with an awareness and acknowledgement that Satan is real. If you believe in good angels, then you should know there are bad angels as well [often called demons] whose sole purpose is to do you harm.[5] Satan is a fallen angel.[6] Being equipped with this awareness that you are under attack is a major step in your long-term preparation for your success and fighting your battles head-on. Friends, you can have no better complete preparation for any battle in your spiritual and personal life that will translate to your business than to put on the *"Full Armor of God."* The apostle Paul gives us a clear, eye-opening, God-inspired blueprint of who is really waging the battle against you, where this battle is fought, and how you can win it in Ephesians 6:10–18, outlined below and discussed in Chapter 12 (Prepared for Spiritual Warfare):

> *Finally, my brethren, be strong in the Lord, and in the power of his might. Put on the whole armor of God, that ye may be able to stand against the wiles of the devil. For we wrestle not against flesh and blood, but against principalities, against powers, against the rulers of the darkness of this world, against spiritual wickedness in high places. Wherefore take unto you the whole armor of God, that ye may be able to withstand in the evil day, and having done all, to stand. Stand therefore, having your loins girt*

about with truth, and having on the breastplate of righteousness; And your feet shod with the preparation of the gospel of peace; Above all, taking the shield of faith, wherewith ye shall be able to quench all the fiery darts of the wicked. And take the helmet of salvation, and the sword of the Spirit, which is the word of God: Praying always with all prayer and supplication in the Spirit, and watching thereunto with all perseverance and supplication for all saints.

Note that the scripture says to be strong <u>in the Lord and the power of His might.</u> It is through God's mighty power that you will be successful in battling the forces against you. <u>Your role</u>, however, is to put on each part of the armor and pray <u>daily</u>. God's armor provides the protection and strength to press forward in battle and live in freedom. By having His Grace and living in freedom, you are empowered to accomplish great things in your walk with Him. The armor protects your spirit, body and soul from satanic darts and arrows like fear, depression, addiction, timidity, guilt, shame, anxiety, indecision, and low self-esteem. God's armor also protects you from sin and sinful conduct, like stealing or an illicit relationship that can result in satan stealing your testimony thereby making you ineffective in fulfilling God's purpose for your life and serving His people. The armor fortifies you completely. 1 Thessalonians 5:23 says: *Now may the God of peace Himself sanctify you completely; and may your whole spirit, soul, and body be preserved blameless at the coming of our Lord Jesus Christ.*

Dealing with the traditional reasons businesses fail like poor marketing, low sales volume or undercapitalization is the easy part. You can learn how to fix those things and generate more sales and profits in other training that I offer. The tough part is preparing you for the long haul and to follow proven strategies for success, as well as face the challenges ahead with confidence, endurance, and excellence. God intends for you to have joy and peace on this journey to the success that awaits you, but it requires preparation, a willing heart, and spiritual growth.

The principles in this book are not on trial. I know they work, as do many successful entrepreneurs, millionaires and spiritual leaders with whom I have talked and studied.[7] What is on trial here is your determination and commitment to you own success and to move beyond your present circumstance. This is about your desire to move into a realm of abundance, freedom, joy and prosperity which God has promised you. God is a big God and has equipped you with very specific gifts to accomplish great things and serve His people. 1 Peter 4:10 says, *Each of you should use whatever gift you have received to serve others, as faithful stewards of God's grace in its various forms.* It is through the vision and direction God places in your heart that you will *receive and achieve* all that awaits you in business as you use your unique gifts.

In the Book of Ecclesiastes King Solomon made a well-documented search for the true meaning of life and found that all we pursue (wisdom, pleasure, substances to alter the mind, materialism, security, authority, etc.) apart from God is meaningless. He summed up his study in Ecclesiastes 12:13, where he says: *Let us hear the conclusion of the whole matter: Fear God, and keep his commandments: for this is the whole duty of man.*

We often tend to forget or ignore the fact that keeping God's commandments is also required in the pursuit of success in business. Entrepreneurs, who have been through the fire and reached the pinnacle of success, follow essentially the same tried-and-true path to get there. Yet, the biblical principles underpinning each step for most is rarely acknowledged. God's presence is evident in the lives of some, and in others, not so evident. Having studied the lives and teachings of numerous people of great success, influence and wealth, plus, in my own experience and study of God's Word with the guidance of the Holy Spirit, I have identified the essential steps that provide a path to joy, success and abundance. I call them the "*7 Universal Steps for Success.*" If these *7 Universal Steps* are studied and implemented by you, they will have an immediate transformational effect on your small business and your life for the better. I arranged these steps after having been inspired by the teachings of many pastors, studied the strategies of business coaches, college professors, marketing and sales experts, including online business gurus. Also, over the years, I met and talked with millionaires, entrepreneurs and business executives of Fortune 500 companies, some of whom started out as small-business owners in dorm rooms and garages. I've read many of their books and studied reports, articles, training programs and all kinds of business systems.[8] All of the successful people I studied are brilliant in one way or another and imbued with many gifts. My conclusion is that success, lasting joy, true purpose and prosperity, are also available to you because these things can be studied, learned and implemented by you. However, to have unending joy and peace that accompanies the success you will attain, you must, as King Solomon says: "Fear God, and keep His commandments."[9]

THE STARTING POINT

In starting this journey, it is important to know and understand that God has chosen you for a specific purpose. In fulfilling that purpose, He promises that you will bear fruit that will last. John 15:16 (NIV) says: *"You did not choose me, but I chose you and appointed you so that you might go and bear fruit – fruit that will last – and so that whatever you ask in my name the Father will give you."* The challenge for each of us is to come to the realization that our time is limited for accomplishing the things God has before us. James 4:14 tells us that our lives are but a *mist that appears for a little while and then vanishes.* It is important that we be as efficient as possible in how we spend our time producing the fruit God desires of us. His instructions on how to do that are found throughout the Bible and He reminds us often that we must be diligent in our work because our time is limited. In Ecclesiastes 9:10, we are instructed: *"Whatever you do, do well. For when you go to the grave, there will be no work or planning or knowledge or wisdom."* I like to call *the Bible God's inspirational time-management system that enables and empowers you, as a believer, to lead the most productive and fruitful life possible during your time on earth which will result in salvation for you and the people you are called to serve and influence.*

To be effective and efficient on this journey, it is important that you not just read about various strategies and formulas that will benefit you. You must also gain a true perspective and view of where you actually stand on this path regarding how productive you've been in the past, but more importantly how productive you will be in the future. Christ often teaches productivity in terms of bearing fruit:

John 15:1-8 (NKJV) reads:

> "I am the true vine, and My Father is the vinedresser. Every branch in Me that does not bear fruit [Level 1, "No Fruit"] He takes away; and every *branch* that bears fruit [Level 2, "Fruit"] He prunes, that it may bear more fruit [Level 3, "More Fruit"]. You are already clean because of the word which I have spoken to you. Abide in Me, and I in you. As the branch cannot bear fruit of itself, unless it abides in the vine, neither can you, unless you abide in Me.
>
> I am the vine, you *are* the branches. He who abides in Me, and I in him, bears much fruit [Level 4, "Much fruit"]; for without Me you can do nothing. If anyone does not abide in Me, he is cast out as a branch and is withered; and they gather them and throw *them* into the fire, and they are burned. If you abide in Me, and My words abide in you, you will ask what you desire, and it shall be done for you. By this

My Father is glorified, that you bear much fruit [Level 4, "Much Fruit"]; so you will be My disciples."

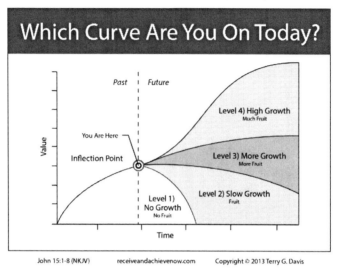

You and your business are on one of the four curves (or paths) shown above.[10] ("No Fruit"= Not Productive; "Fruit" = Productive; "More Fruit"= Highly Productive; "Much Fruit" = Wildly Productive) The bottom plane represents "Time." The "Time" could be a day, week, month, year or even your lifetime. The left vertical plane represents "Value." "Value" could be dollars or the quality of relationships with your spouse, family, boss, church members or effectiveness as a leader, volunteer, or influencer for Christ, etc. For a business "Value" represents sales revenue. The "Inflection Point" represents the present. It is where the past ends and the future begins. This chart allows you to reflect upon your past experiences plus it gives you a snapshot and peep into the future path your life or business will be taking. It helps you to realize there are things you must take control of and do if you want to produce much fruit or generate high levels of revenue. So the question for you is: "Am I putting things in place that will ensure I will be fruitful going forward, starting at this very moment?" As you examine your past, ask this question of yourself: "Will I allow the experiences and difficulties of my past to limit my future growth and be an excuse not to improve my life and help others? The problem for most who bear no-fruit and are not productive is fear of failure and rejection. That's because they incorrectly focus on the failures and the pain of the past rather than believing God's Word which specifically tells us that those so called failures are designed to make us stronger and better equipped for the future challenges. James 1:2-3 (NIV) tells us to: *"Consider it pure joy, my brothers and sisters, whenever you face trials of many kinds, because you know that the testing of your faith produces perseverance.* So, the answer to the question is you must use the experiences of the past, no matter what they are, as a source of strength and motivation to propel you to high levels of productivity and fruit bearing. Your focus must be on the many positive things and successes that brought you to this point today.

The fact that you are reading this book and seeking more is a testament that there have been many successes in your life. Examples include: successes with your family; successes with personal accomplishments over the years; successes that are work- or job-related; things you have learned; challenges that you have persevered through despite opposition; success with things you faced that no one even knew you were going through, but you got through it or you are even handling it right now. These are all very significant successes and character- building victories that are the foundation for even greater success. You were made for a purpose and to bear much fruit. Bearing fruit, is the metaphor Christ used to teach His disciples about creating value in their lives and being productive in their service to Him. The fruit you bear most often is manifested through your special gifts or talents and includes things you enjoy doing or are naturally drawn to. Your fruit may also come through in things you have a passion for or a special skill in doing. The secret to being productive, He taught, was that we "abide" in Him (i.e. " fear God and keep his commandments"[11]) (If you love me, keep my commands."[12]) You may understand what it means to "abide" in the spiritual sense, but what does it mean to "abide" in your personal life and business dealings?

- It means recognizing first that you are a steward of all you earn. (Luke 12:48)
- It means committing your plans to God and trusting in Him to bring them to pass. (Psalm 37:5)
- It means giving back a portion of that with which He has entrusted you. (Proverbs 3:9-10)
- It means never sacrificing people over profits and being fair in your pricing. (Psalm 112:5-7)
- It means being a person of integrity when dealing with customers. (Deuteronomy 25:13-16, NIV; Proverbs 11:20, NLT)
- It means paying fair wages and treating all employees with respect. (Jeremiah 22:13)

- It means seeking "win-win" agreements with suppliers and doing unto others as you would have them to do unto you. (Luke 6:31)
- It means not becoming overly burdened by debt. (Proverbs 22:7)
- It means becoming wiser about negotiations and contracts so the unscrupulous will not take advantage of you. (1 Corinthians 3:18).
- It means understand what you are getting into. Count the cost. (Luke 14:28)
- It means praying to God for wisdom to guide you in your every move. (Proverbs 3:13-14)
- It means being diligent and resourceful with the talents the Master has entrusted to you because God expects you to earn a profit from those talents and not sit on them or "bury them in the ground. (Matthew 25:14-30)

The great bonus in "abiding," according the scripture is, when we are successful in our work and producing much fruit, God is "glorified"! How cool is that! God created work before there was sin. (Genesis 2:15) He instructed Adam and Eve to *"Be fruitful and multiply and fill the earth and subdue it and have dominion over the fish and of the sea and over the birds of the heavens and over every living thing that moves on the earth."* Genesis 1:28. As we abide in God, we honor Him when we work and are fruitful on our jobs and in the businesses we start and grow.

Duane P. Donner, II, the originator of the Inflection Point chart above, who allowed me to "tweak" it to represent growth in terms of John 15 fruit production is himself a great example of "abiding" in Jesus Christ. Duane is the CEO of Founder's Forum, an investment banking firm that operates in the high-powered world of buying and selling businesses, generally up to and in the $50 million range. Despite interacting with people daily where being Christ-like is the last thing on their minds, Duane thrives. First, when you enter his office in Birmingham, among the usual array of business magazines are inspirational books that provide guidance and encouragement based on the Gospel of Jesus Christ. In addition, he gives every person who works for him a book entitled *"A Light Shines Bright in Babylon* by Buck Jacobs. It's a wonderful quick read about making your work your ministry. Duane requires his team to exhibit integrity in all their dealings with their clients. These qualities are paying dividends for Duane's company and business is booming for him as evidenced by the many satisfied clients he has. Duane is producing "much fruit" in his business and glorifying God in the process.

THE 7 UNIVERSAL STEPS FOR SUCCESS

Having touched on the importance of spending time and doing what it takes to become highly productive, you are now ready for the *7 Universal Steps* every small- business owner needs to take his or her business to the next level. These 7 Universal Steps are foundational to providing a lasting framework for success for you and your business. The steps which follow are seeds ready to be planted on the good ground of your mind. God will provide the increase which will bring great success and much fruit. Matthew 13:23 says, *"But he who received seed on the good ground is he who hears the word and understands it, who indeed bears fruit and produces: some a hundredfold, some sixty, some thirty."*

It is with a solid foundation built on the Word of God and the strategies found in the following 15 chapters that Jesus Christ will radically transform your life and businesses. The secret is to be intentional in embracing these 7 steps because the outcome is wealth creation, more influence, and a transformation in your personal and spiritual development. It is this transformation that will turn the number of small-business failures into success story after success story. In your own business you will see change, become stronger and wiser as you begin to focus on the important things necessary to build, grow and scale your business that will lead to greater joy, peace, prosperity and success God has promised. Utilizing these steps you will become a more self-confident and highly sought after entrepreneur, so let's get started:

Step 1. <u>Develop an Effective Prayer Life</u>: The most valuable time you can spend to ensure your success is to develop an effective prayer life with your Heavenly Father. Having an *effective prayer life* is the starting point for any small-business owner to get on the fast track to a life of abundance and joy. It is your connection to the True Source of your strength, protection and true success.[13] God is the One who made you for a purpose and gave you gifts and talents to fulfill that purpose, so why wouldn't you want to connect with

Him? God's Word tells us that we are to pray on all occasions.[14] An effective prayer life is the principle secret that will provide a spiritual covering and constant connection with God as you implement the remaining six steps for success that you are about to learn below. Christian Bible teacher and author Joyce Meyer succinctly tells you how to get an effective prayer life in her best-selling book entitled, *Battlefield of the Mind,* when she says:

> "If you want to have an effective prayer life, develop a good personal relationship with the Father. Know He loves you, that He is full of mercy, that He will help you. Get to know Jesus. He is your Friend. He died for you. Get to know the Holy Spirit. He is with you all the time as your Helper. Let Him help you."[15]

An effective prayer life with your Heavenly Father is all about relationship. How do you develop a relationship with the Father? The same way you develop a relationship with your earthly father, mother or guardian. You spend time with them. You talk with them. You interact with them. You take your problems to them. In the case of your Heavenly Father, you praise Him; you study and meditate on His Holy Word; you obey his commands; you place your trust in Him. You put Him first in everything you do. You are God's child and developing a relationship with Him entitles you to ask what you may and the scripture says, it will be given to you.[16]

Developing an effective prayer life will do many amazing things for you, but here are two that will put you on the track to an abundant life.

1) It gives you access to wisdom. You gain wisdom in two ways: a) through life's experiences over time; and, b) directly from God. The problem with wisdom from life's experiences is that though it can be useful and even insightful, it is skewed with the human biases and frailties you have; it takes many years to acquire; and it grows out of the Tree of Knowledge. On the other hand, wisdom from God is instant; it brings riches, honor and joy; it's more valuable than gold and silver, it gives you access to the Tree of Life; and, it's how God founded the earth. [Proverbs 3:13-24 (NKJV)] [An excellent resource on the Tree of Life, *Fresh Air*, Chris Hodges, Tyndall House Publishers] You've heard the saying: *"He [she] is wise beyond his [her] years"*. Wisdom enhances your decision-making process; it provides you with knowledge and speeds up learning; it gives you discernment; it enables you to understand things you may not have experienced, but are nevertheless able to make prudent decisions regarding those things. Wisdom is an amazing gift from God. It is both a multiplier and accelerator. If you want to see exponential growth in <u>any</u> area of your life, pray for God to grant you wisdom. This is what King Solomon asked for when God said to him, *"Ask for whatever you want me to give you."* Solomon did not ask for riches or wealth, he asked for wisdom. (2 Chronicles 1:7-12)

2) It protects your mind. Do you realize how much your mind is under attack from negative influences in the course of a

24-day? How can you make good decisions if you are constantly bombarded with negative information designed to appeal strictly to worldly human desires that influence you in ways which are often unhealthy? Or, on the other extreme, what about information and circumstances that cause stress on a daily basis? Things like negative news and media reports, personal financial challenges, difficulties on the job, not having a job, problems with school, a personal health challenge, strained relationships with loved ones, or the challenges of caring for an aging parent or a special needs child. In many situations, people are numb to the pain in addressing the challenges because dealing with it becomes a part of daily routines. People also are most often unaware of the negative influence on their minds of being connected to technology 24/7. (See book, *The Digital Invasion*, Dr. Archabold Hart and Dr. Sylvia Hart Frejd) But there can be joy and peace in the midst of these things. God, through His Son Jesus Christ wants you to trust Him and bring all of the challenges and difficulties to Him. Nothing compares to His embrace and how He can bring clarity to every situation through His grace and love for you. [Proverbs 3:5-6; Matthew 11:28–30 (NIV); Matthew 6:34]

You need a mind that is clear and which has the ability to focus on the right things and stay focused on them. You need a mind that can break through the clutter, tell you, at any moment, what's important and what's not important, then instruct you to put aside the fear and take action! You need a mind that can control your emotions and not allow your emotions to control you. [For example, someone darts out in front of you and takes a parking spot you were waiting for. What do you do? OK. What you don't' do is pull a gun out of the glove compartment. Christ, who died for you, has given you the capacity to calmly handle that situation and much more. Christ needs you for more important things than to chastise a knucklehead. You can pray for him, however.

Step 2. <u>Imagine and Commit to Your Success</u>: You must first imagine your success, then have an absolutely unwavering commitment to achieving it. Let me start with some tough love here. First, you need to imagine bigger and dream bigger. That begins with breaking the routine, mundane, mediocre way of thinking that has shaped has your past. God wants you to give Him your best. Don't judge yourself by mediocre standards other people exhibit. Look for role models who are excelling in your areas of interest. Look for people who have a heart for God and for service. You are important to God's plans. He made you for a purpose which includes leading a life of abundance so that you will grow in influence and change the world around you. But you'll never get there unless you set your mind and goals on higher things that will put you in a place of abundance. God has placed a calling on your life do great things. Use your imagination to envision what it feels like to be successful, prosperous, have influence, respect and joy. It can be yours. Imagine also the steps you must take and things you must do to make your journey to an abundant life a reality. Abraham was initially reluctant and doubtful when faced with the prospect of what it meant to become "the father of many nations." But Abraham used his imagination and *called those things that did not exist as though* *they did exist* before they became a reality as God had promised in His covenant with Abraham. In Romans 4:17 we find these words:

> *As it is written, "I have made you a father of many nations" in the presence of Him whom he believed – God, who gives life to the dead and <u>calls those things which do not exist as though they did.</u>"*

Pause and take a moment right now to imagine the success you desire, including the things you need to be freed from. Permanently affix in your and memory what that success feels like. Relying on God's Word, you are *calling those things that do not exist as though they do* and putting yourself one step closer to them becoming a reality. Write out what success feels like for you in a short statement. Make a separate list of the things you want to be freed from (which you will turn over to God).

Once you imagine your success, you must commit and maintain a relentless dedication to attain that success. This is a common trait of highly successful people and it fuels them every day. You must maintain that commitment and believe in your heart that with God's help you can and will become that successful person. Success does not happen by accident. It comes by intentional thinking and action.

You must maintain a passion and desire for success. The drive and determination to be successful must be ever present on your heart and on your mind. Many others have done it and so can you. Your actions everyday must be steadfast toward the attainment of goals that will bring you the success you desire. Imagine what you will look like once you become the success you know you can be and that God wants you to be. Becoming successful in your business and generating wealth empowers you to be an even greater instrument for doing God's works.

You must be innovative in facing the challenges you are sure to encounter. You must not allow minor setbacks or discouraging circumstances to deter you or eat away at your commitment to your success. You must develop an attitude that does not fear rejection and be willing to persist in the face of it. Don't take rejection personally. There is always a bright side and lessons to be learned from rejection. Always speak blessings on yourself. Always encourage yourself, in the Lord.

Let everything about you and the plans you have indicate you *expect* to be successful and for God to prosper you. Expectancy is a good thing and a measure of your faith. Psalm 5:3 (NKJV) says: *In the morning, Lord, you hear my voice; in the morning I lay my requests before you and wait expectantly.*

Finally, don't let the enormity of the task before you or your present circumstances deter you imagining what success feels like. Neither the tasks or circumstances are too big for God. The biblical story of the servant of Abraham, who was given the monumental task of traveling over a thousand miles to a foreign land to find a wife for Abraham's son, Isaac, is the perfect example of commitment and not allowing circumstance overwhelm you. The servant accepted and embarked on his arduous task, but to ensure success of the plan which he imagined, the servant committed his plan to God in prayer. The scripture in Genesis 24:12–19 tells us that the servant was indeed successful and found Rebekah who became the wife of Isaac. So, by prayer and action, the servant was committed to his success.

Understand and know that when you commit your plan to the Lord and trust in Him, you are committing to your success and He will bring it to pass.[17]

Step 3: <u>Be Willing To Learn And Create Value For Others</u>. You must constantly be willing to learn. Are you willing to learn new things or enhance your current skills? The answer is you must be willing to learn in order to grow. Learning is an investment in yourself and that's how it should be viewed. You must have a teachable spirit and willingness to absorb new knowledge and apply it. Ask yourself, is my mind closed to learning new things? Of course, you have to be honest with yourself. Here a newsflash! Everything you need to be successful and prosperous can be learned. Plus, you don't have to be a rocket scientist to do it. But, you must develop a thirst for learning and desire to uplift yourself. The knowledge you gain is empowering and draws people and wealth-generating opportunities to you. Read books, do research online and offline, sign up for webinars and teleseminars, read blogs, find a mentor or coach, take a course – become an expert and authority on what you do best. Study from the top people in the field you are in or area you are interested in. Learn from them. Proverbs 1:5 says: *"Let the wise listen and add to their learning, and let the discerning get guidance."* Even Jesus, in His humanity as a young boy grew in learning. Luke 2:52 says, *"And Jesus increased in wisdom and* *stature, and in favor with God and man."* When you learn and increase in knowledge, you are increasing your ability to give to others and create great value for them. When you create value for others, many biblical principle of giving and wealth creation go to work for you. For example Proverbs 11:25 (NIV) says: *A generous person will prosper. Whoever refreshes others will be refreshed.*

You must also be willing to learn what God's Word teaches about wealth creation, money and debt. You must increase your money IQ. Proverbs 22:7 says: *"Rich people rule over those who are poor. Borrowers are slaves to lenders."* The lesson here is if you want financial freedom, avoiding debt is key. For every debt you eliminate, you automatically create wealth that moves you closer to financial freedom.

Also, money is not evil. What the scripture says in 1 Timothy 6:10 is that it's the "love" of money that's evil and the bad things people do as a result of the "love" of money. A person with a healthy mindset about money and wealth can do great things in service to God. It's not about how much you make. It's about how much you keep that increases your wealth and influence. Save, pay cash and invest in things that are considered assets (that go up in value or don't drain money from you bank account). Avoid creating liabilities. (Liabilities drain your cash) Buying things on credit creates liabilities.

Step 4: Be Willing To Change. You must be open and willing to *change.* Change is never easy and it's sometimes scary. But if you want to grow as a person and move to new heights, change is absolutely necessary. You must examine the things that cause you resist change and eliminate them. All of us have resisted change at some point in our lives and that includes you. When you look inside and ask yourself why are you resistant to change you will find the number one reason is procrastination. It's easier to simply put it off until another day. The most dangerous word in the dictionary that is a threat to your success, to abundance and even salvation is *tomorrow*. *"Tomorrow" is a tool of satan.* Proverbs 27:1 says: *"Do not boast about tomorrow, for you do not know what a day may bring."* Other reasons are fear, complacency, lack of knowledge and lack of self-confidence. Think of the people you already know that will not change, even if their lives depended upon it. However, once you take that first step to change and put on the *"new man"*, God is ready to favor you as one who is walking in His image. Colossians 3:9-10 (NKJV) says: *"Do not lie to one another, since you have put off the old man with his deeds, ^{10} and have put on the new man who is renewed in knowledge according to the image of Him who created him."*

One of the greatest examples of change and transformation in the Bible and putting on the new man is given in Acts 9:1-9 and Acts 9:20 regarding Saul's encounter with God on the Damascus road. Saul had been a fervent persecutor of Christians, but once he *learned* the truth, he changed his name to Paul and became one of the most prolific evangelists for Jesus Christ and spreading the Gospel.

Step 5: <u>Be Willing To Implement Change</u>. Being "willing to change" is not enough. You must actually *implement* the change in your life to attain the success you desire. In other words, stop making excuses and take action. You must trust in God, step out on faith and implement the change that is necessary to improve your life and move you beyond your present circumstance. Proverbs 3:5-6 says: Trust in the LORD with all your heart, And lean not on your own understanding; In all your ways acknowledge Him, And He shall direct your paths.

Studies show that the speed at which you take action to implement change has a direct correlation to the levels of success you attain in reaching your goals.[18] If you act promptly to implement change, the results you desire come more quickly. You should know that many people acquire knowledge. But in addition to acquiring knowledge, you must learn from that knowledge, be willing to change, then implement that change. Andrew Carnegie was noted for saying that those who are slow to make up their minds are equally slow in carrying out [implementing] their decisions.[19] In other words, the longer you take to implement change, the more likely it is you will never implement the change necessary to improve your present circumstance. Albert Einstein once said: *"The definition of insanity is doing the same thing over and over again and expecting a different result."* This is almost the same phrase which can be used to define fear. That is, *doing the same thing over and over again <u>because you are afraid of</u> a different result.* In other words, when you are hesitant or slow to implement change that is beneficial for you, it is very likely you are fearful of the new result that places new things before you which are likely outside of your comfort zone. When God puts a "new song" in your mouth, it's there to bless you. It is there to change how you think, how you act, and what you proclaim. You must conquer any fear, trust in God, and implement the change. God will carry you safely through as you implement the change. Consider the words of Psalm 40:2-4 (NIV):

> *He lifted me out of the slimy pit, out of the mud and mire; he set my feet on a rock and gave me a firm place to stand. He put a new song in my mouth, a hymn of praise to our God. Many will see and fear the LORD and put their trust in him. Blessed is the one who trusts in the LORD, who does not look to the proud, to those who turn aside to false gods.*

Don't let what people think of you or what you fear hold you back from doing things differently. Your concern should be to satisfy the only audience that matters in this life, which is an audience of One. Study God's Word. It will change you and give you the courage to implement positive change in your business and in your life.

Here again, the Apostle Paul is a great example of one who was not only "willing to change" after his encounter with Christ and learning the truth, he actually took action to *implement change.* These changes included being the author of nearly half of the books in the New Testament, starting several churches and spreading the Gospel across the Roman Empire, Asia Minor and Europe, including the Church at Corinth.[20] Paul did not develop amnesia after his encounter with Christ, as many of us do, and revert back to his old ways. He became a believer, accepted his mission and implemented every detail of that mission until his last breath.

Understand, however, you don't implement change just for the sake of making change. The change must have a purpose. You must be guided by sound spiritual doctrine. Otherwise, you can become frustrated and get bounced around like tumbleweed, chasing every new thing that blows your way. Ephesians 4:14 teaches us:

Till we all come to the unity of the faith and of the knowledge of the Son of God, to a perfect man, to the measure of the stature of the fullness of Christ; that we should no longer be children, tossed to and fro and carried about with every wind of doctrine, by the trickery of men, in the cunning craftiness of deceitful plotting, but, speaking the truth in love, may grow up in all things into Him who is the head – Christ –.

Step 6: <u>Be Self-Motivated</u>: You have to motivate yourself when you don't feel motivated. Allow your passion to motivate you and provide the energy you need. That's why it's vitally important that you set your goals on things you care for and get excited about. Things you enjoy doing. That's what enables you to energize yourself when you feel you don't have enough energy. You need energy, vigor and vitality on this journey. The awesome thing is you don't have to rely on your own strength to create this energy. Isaiah 40:31 (NIV) tells us: *"But those who hope in the LORD will renew their strength. They will soar on wings like eagles; they will run and not grow weary, they will walk and not be faint."*

Link your motivation to your purpose and life goals. Are you motivated to move beyond your present circumstance? Do you have desire to impact people's lives, be a success story or leave a meaningful legacy? Are you motivated to achieve because of your children, spouse or family? Or perhaps it's to serve God's purposes? Whatever your purpose and motivation is, keep it in the forefront of your mind and allow it to be the fuel that gives you that motivation and drive.

In rebuilding the Wall of Jerusalem, Nehemiah understood the value of having his men to be self-motivated and having the right motivation in protecting their efforts against imminent attack. Consider his strategy:

> *Therefore I stationed some of the people behind the lowest points of the wall at the exposed places, posting them by families, with their swords, spears and bows. After I looked things over, I stood up and said to the nobles, the officials and the rest of the people, "Don't be afraid of them. Remember the Lord, who is great and awesome, and fight for your families, your sons and your daughters, your wives and your homes."*
>
> Nehemiah 4:13-14

The key to your success is your ability to link whatever motivates you to something that is important enough and close enough to your heart to provide you with a consistently high level of energy to move you to persistent action toward your goals.

Step 7. Be Self-Confident. How you feel about yourself and how you see yourself has everything to do with the levels of success you will attain. This is a key secret to success. That's why it is critical for you to be your own best friend, have good thoughts and *God thoughts* about yourself. When you feel good about yourself and see yourself as being successful, your thoughts and actions project positively into the things you do and to the people with whom you interact. The most important thing here is to understand and know that you are a child of God who loves you unconditionally and is with you through every challenge you face and every fear you have.

Self-confidence is also equated with self-esteem or what you think about yourself. You should always think good thoughts about yourself. Have an expectation that good things and blessings are going to come your way because you are a child of God. God has a role for you in His wonderful master plan. I can assure you, it is not a small plan and your role is not a small role. There are people He wants you to touch and influence. God wants you to live an abundant life because the more abundance and influence you have, the more people you can reach. God wants you in the game. It should help you to know that the confidence you have can be built upon to give you more self-confidence. <u>You can learn to be self-confident by studying His Word and reaching out to help others.</u> That's why you must always think positive thoughts about yourself, speak blessings on yourself and encourage yourself in the Lord, <u>daily</u>. These things will make you a powerful self-confident force in everything you do.

Do This Simple Exercise to Build Your Self-Confidence:

Every night before bed, clear your mind and recite the following scriptures to yourself, and recite them again every morning: *"I am a child of God"* (John 1:12) *"I am free from condemnation"* (Romans 8: 1-2) ; *I am "strong in the Lord"* (Ephesians 6:10) *"I have been chosen and appointed to bear fruit"* (John 15:16); I can do all things through Christ who strengthens me. (Philippians 4:13 NJKV). Meditate on these words and see how God will move to increase and restore your self-confidence.

Read more about self-confidence in Chapter 9.

BECOME A BREAKTHROUGH THINKER

This book is not about giving you temporary economic tips here and there. It's about teaching you life-changing, business and financial-empowerment strategies that will serve as a guide for success based on God's precepts. To be successful requires that you become a breakthrough thinker. You must be able to envision success and victory and be able to chart a path to it. You must be able to unplug from the negative influences around you that generate fear and doubt, and take action. You must be prepared to go against "conventional wisdom" and tap into "God's wisdom" for direction. It is all about a self-awareness that you are thinking for yourself and being guided by the Holy Spirit. So, how do you become a breakthrough thinker? Here are the secrets:

- **First** – *Praise God for blessing you with gifts to do great things.* The fact that you are seeking more now and reading this book says you already have what it takes to enlarge your territory as Jabez prayed in 1 Chronicles 4:10, and become the success you desire. Your gifts will attract the people and resources you need, and God will open doors as your gifts are utilized. Proverbs 18:16 (NIV) says: *A gift opens the way and ushers the giver into the presence of the great.*

- **Second** – *Meditate on God's Word. Get in alignment with God's Word.* Claim the success and prosperity He has promised.

Keep this Book of the Law always on your lips; meditate on it day and night, so that you may be careful to do everything written in it. Then you will be prosperous and successful. (Joshua 1:8, NIV)

- **Third** – *Pray for wisdom, discernment, and good judgment.* The more of it you have, the more others will seek you out.

Happy is the man who finds wisdom, And the man who gains understanding; For her proceeds are better than the profits of silver, And her gain than fine gold. (Proverbs 3:13–14, NKJV)

- **Fourth** – _Seek the guidance of the Holy Spirit_. It will keep you in God's Will, moving in the right direction.

But the Advocate, the Holy Spirit, whom the Father will send in my name, will teach you all things and will remind you of everything I have said to you. (John 14:26, ASV)

- **Fifth** –_ Be innovative and operate continuously in faith outside your comfort zone._ That's when and where the breakthrough takes place!

For I know the plans I have for you," declares the LORD, "plans to prosper you and not to harm you, plans to give you hope and a future. (Jeremiah 29:11)

- **Sixth** – _Never take no for an answer_. There is always another way, and more often, a better way! Why take their word for it? Be persistent.

Jesus replied, What is impossible with man is possible with God[21] (Luke 18:27).

- **Seventh** –_Expect a breakthrough_. Expectancy is a demonstration of your faith that God will bring about change in your life.

And, behold, a woman, which was diseased with an issue of blood twelve years, came behind him, and touched the hem of his garment: For she said within herself, If I may but touch his garment, I shall be whole. (Matthew 9:20-21)

We are all blessed that God sent us the perfect example in the person of Jesus Christ to show us how to be successful in our personal lives and in business. While no human can ever be perfect, joy and success is ours for the taking if we become more Christ-like in our business dealings with others and in our personal lives. The Gospel contains a wealth of enduring strategies and principles, which, if believed and followed, can lead to untold influence, and prosperity. This is in God's Word. Please understand, however, that when I speak of success and prosperity, I am not necessarily talking about money or instant riches. I would not limit God in that way and neither should you. This book, is about much more than that. It's about preparing you for a journey and establishing a path that will lead and sustain you as you seek and receive *all* the blessings God has in store for you. There are many people with money, but they have no joy, peace, or real success. Just look around at some of the wealthy celebrity types and personalities you hear and read about every day.

As you study and employ these business and biblical principles, your vision and how to attain the success you desire will come into focus. You may even be surprised at the level of joy you will find on your journey. The principles and strategies in this book are based on the highest grossing best-seller of all time, the Holy Bible. These principles have worked for millions and I am confident they will work for you. The amazing thing, however, is you don't have to wait until some distant time in the future for the benefits outlined in this book to take effect. The benefits are available to you right now if you make a decision and choose to implement them today! And that's no sales puffing. If you turn in your Bible to Mark 10:29–30, (or call it up on your smartphone or mobile device) you'll find these words:

So Jesus answered and said, "Assuredly, I say to you, there is no one who has left house or brothers or sisters or father or mother or wife or children or lands, for My sake and the gospel's, who shall not receive a hundredfold **now in this time** – *houses and brothers and sisters and mothers and children and lands, with persecutions – and in the age to come, eternal life."*

I emphasized four words in this scripture, *"now in this time."* When you choose and follow Jesus Christ, His promise is to bless you *"now in this time!"* That means today, not next year, or five years from now, but today.

I thank God for receiving this Word from a recorded sermon preached by Bishop T.D. Jakes. I listened to this sermon while driving to a Visionary Leadership Conference hosted by Pastor Jesse Duplantis in New Orleans. Amazingly, Pastor Duplantis preached on the same subject my first day at the conference. His central theme was about claiming and receiving Christ's blessings right now! Though I already had a title for this book, I was moved to change it, and add the word "Now!" I can only describe it as God breathing new life into it because the pages seem to dance with an enhanced level of excitement as I re-read them in the context of the new title. It fit perfectly. *Receive and Achieve . . . Now!*

I'm excited, so immediately following my prayer for you, let's get started!

Most gracious Father, I thank You for all those who are reading the pages of this book. I pray that each person will be touched, encouraged, and empowered by Your Holy Word and the words herein, which You have placed on my heart to write. I pray each person receives from You, wisdom, joy, peace, abundance and the endurance to overcome the challenges ahead with excitement and an expectancy that You will prosper their plans and bless each one with an abundance of success. I pray that You touch every need right now, bless and protect their families and loved ones. Finally, I pray that Your favor will continually be upon each person as You open doors for them in business and in their personal lives, which no one can close. In the mighty name of Jesus Christ, Amen!

—*Terry G. Davis, JD, MBA,*
SmartBizUniversity.com™, Founder
The 90-Day Abundant Life Challenge™
www.90DayALC.com
Montgomery, Alabama

http://receiveandachievenow.com/introduction

PART II.
FINDING YOUR TRUE CALLING AND SETTING THE PATH

God created me for a purpose and to make a difference in this world. Despite frequent distractions and challenges, I will maintain my focus on doing God's will for me. I will seek to stay in His will and to do good works because once in His will, nothing on earth can keep His purpose for me from being fulfilled, including having the abundant life He has promised His followers. All things work together for good to those who love the Lord and are called according to His purpose.

I love you God!

Reference:

Isaiah 14:24

Romans 8:31–39

Romans 8:28

Chapter 1

VISION

Where there is no vision, the people perish.

Proverbs 29:18

SECRET #1: SUCCESSFUL ENTREPRENEURS HAVE VISION

Are you running your business without a vision? In business, just as in life, you must have vision to provide purpose and direction for where you want to go. But where does vision come from? It comes from the calling God places on your heart. That calling says to you that you have a purpose in life and a desire to achieve, be successful, to serve and lead. Through that calling and your dreams, God enables you to envision what you can become, the kind of abundant life you can lead and what you can do to make the lives of others better. The things you envision are often beyond anything you could have conceived or can imagine is possible. But that's how God works. He is God of the universe and so His plans are naturally (supernaturally, that is) beyond what you can possibly come up with on your own. However, you a special part of His plans and the gifts He has given you are there for you to be a fully engaged participant, in a big way, in fulfilling the purpose for which you were uniquely created. Ecclesiastes 9:10 says: "Whatever your hand finds to do, do it with all your might." He allows you to see and do things that will inspire others to support the vision He has placed in you, whatever that vision is. God has given you the blueprint along with unique and special gifts to make your vision and dreams a reality.

Vision is a word that we should all get excited about. It has an empowering effect on those who are able to effectively *"receive"* and articulate their vision, which enables a person to *"achieve"* great things. Vision is the driving force that motivates a person to boldly step out to reach his or her goals. With a clear vision, you can see where you want to go, see the steps it will take to get there, and anticipate challenges you will face in reaching your goals.

Vision is the compass that sets the direction from which everything else flows for your business. It is your blueprint for life and for your business. Vision sets the framework of how you choose to live and the kind of aspirations you have, your priorities and where you spend your time. We live our lives based on how we view ourselves in the context of expectations we have as shaped by our vision of the future. If your vision provides no hope of a better future when present circumstances are already bleak, you tend to live out your life that way. However, when you have a vision that is clear, it provides hope and purpose. That vision then creates an unstoppable motivating force within you that can move you to a new job, create a new business, develop a new invention, become the architect of massive skyscrapers, take human performance to new heights, inspire you to great leadership, change the world, and more. Everything in our culture and civilization has emanated from the gift of vision. It's been said the two most important days in your life are the day you were born and the day you find out why.[22] Once you know God's purpose in your life and the vision He has planted inside you, you become an awesome force for good with the ability to affect positive change beyond what you could even imagine. The key is knowing that you are a part of something greater and more important than you are and tapping into that that Infinite Source which is able to bring all things to pass. With God as your source, nothing can stop you. *Isaiah 14:24 says: The LORD Almighty has sworn, "Surely, as I have planned, so it will be, and as I have purposed, so it will happen.*

When Glenn Farrington, the president of Digital Seas International, came to me in 1998, he had recently lost his job at AOL and was living with his in-laws. Earlier in his career, Glenn performed comedy on a cruise ship. During that time, he remembered being frustrated at the high cost of calling from the cruise ship to monitor his stocks. Glenn, for years had an urge to go into business for himself. Not having a job gave him more time to think about his future. He found a job, but he had a vision of starting a company to develop a technology that cruise ships around the world could use to connect to the Internet.

As his general counsel and business strategist, I incorporated Digital Seas International for Glenn in Montgomery, Alabama, in 1998. I also helped him develop a business plan and get his first bank loan from First Tuskegee Bank. Using local techies, Glenn developed the technology to connect to the Internet, but which also had the signal strength to hold a stable signal from a cruise ship to a satellite. We built an awesome team and a savvy board of directors that provided a significant brain trust to guide the business. About a year later, we were announcing the signing of a contract I had negotiated with a major satellite provider to offer – for the first time ever – Internet Café service to commercial cruise lines. We moved the company from Montgomery to Miami. Carnival was the first cruise line to deploy the service on the *Royal Princess.* It was a big hit, to say the least. We soon rolled the service out to other cruise lines, including Disney, Holland America, Norwegian, and others. The company was sold and today, a majority of cruise lines that operate in the U.S. still use this service as well as many cruise lines in Europe.[23] It was the power of Glenn's vision that empowered him to motivate a team of people to move to Miami and change the landscape of the cruise line industry.

The same opportunity to achieve great things is available to you as it was to Glenn Farrington. You *can* ignite your vision and establish your goals. Spend time meditating on God's Word, examine your gifts and see how He has specially equipped you to do the work before you. You will find that there are people all around you who can help you, but God will send you many more. While you are meditating and waiting for God to direct you, get busy in a church or ministry performing good deeds. Your vision will become clearer much sooner.

At my seminars on leadership, when I ask people to define vision, I get a variety of responses, such as:

- the ability to see
- to envision yourself in the future
- the ability to comprehend the future
- foresight
- to dream
- the ability to see your goals – imagination in action.

Each of these is correct and captures some portion of what it means to have vision. Indeed, without the visionary and spiritually anointed leadership of many of the founding fathers, the United States would not have been able to draft a Declaration of Independence and Constitution that has endured for more than two hundred years. It is clearly the divine guidance of God that has allowed our nation to be prosperous land it is.

A SIXTH SENSE

Vision works in a myriad of ways. All of us have a measure of vision, but it must be nurtured. To be effective, we must be attuned to our gift of vision. In many ways, vision is like a "sixth sense." It is an innate and intuitive ability to comprehend and process things and information that you can't necessarily see. As adults, we often ask the question, "What is your gut telling you?" You've heard the phrase, "A woman's intuition is always right." This is really the gift of vision God has placed in you. Your mind is processing all the information you know about a situation, to give you the answer, through the Holy Spirit. When you rely on Proverbs 3:5–6 that says: *"Trust in the Lord with all your heart and lean not unto thy own understanding, In all thy ways acknowledge Him and He will direct thy path,"* you've got a "sixth sense" that will get you through any situation.

For many years, I taught a martial arts bible study for youths and teens. One example I gave to demonstrate how to use this "sixth sense" is this: You go into a room, to a party, or even to a playground just to have fun. When you arrive you notice out of the corner of your eye a group of kids doing something, but you can't see what it is. You begin to have a feeling that something is not right about what they are doing. I taught them not to ignore that feeling. That's your "sixth sense" providing you with a warning. It's an awareness upon which you must learn to act. You learn to get away from that situation before something occurs to draw you into it. When you respond, you are using your gift of vision. If you know anything about the comic book and movie character, Spiderman, it's similar to his "Spidey sense." Proverbs 22:3 puts it this way: *"A prudent person foresees danger and takes precautions. The simpleton goes blindly on and suffers the consequences."* Using vision as a sixth sense can be an invaluable tool in your quest for success. Combined with wisdom, using the gift of vision will accelerate the time spent moving toward your goals because you avoid, not only the pitfalls, but the time it takes to recover from the pitfalls and get back on course.

When it comes to business and using vision as a "sixth sense," successful people also take it to another level. They use vision as a motivating tool of empowerment and a vehicle for reaching their goals but they must provide a roadmap for getting there. John Maxwell says *"Anyone can steer the ship, but it takes a leader to chart the course."*[24] Success requires that you be a leader with a vision. The vision you have will generate energy to focus your plans and make them become a reality. Desire and passion will feed into your vision, move you to action and inspire others to join in, as you "chart the course."

TRY THIS EXERCISE

Take a moment right now to envision where you want to be in one year, then three years, and then five years from now. Whether you are working for someone, self-employed, unemployed, or in any type of business, think about the better life you want to have for yourself and family. Write down the things you desire. The important point here is that you must start envisioning yourself where you want to go and the kind of income or revenue you see yourself making. (For some people, it may be a better job or promotion.) Imagine the kind of successful entrepreneur you will become. What kind of house do you want? What kind of clothes will you wear? How much are you giving back to God, your church and the community? What will your life be like five years from now? Everyone loves a winner. But the first person who must believe and see you as a winner is *you*. Now that you are five years out and very successful, think back on the type of things you had to do to become that successful and respected person. Write those things down. Examine everything you have written and include it when you start making plans to develop who you now know you can become. A better life is out there, but getting there has to start with you.

Once you envision where you want to go or what you want to achieve in your business, a transformation takes place in your belief system. Relying on the Holy Spirit, you begin to formulate and develop plans to make your goals and vision a reality. Vision also requires a measure of discipline. As you develop your plans, commit them to God, trust in Him, and He will bring them to pass. [25] Remember that God does not only give you the vision, He gives you the provision to make it happen.

You must have a constant vision of where you want to take your business and you must be able to communicate that vision to others. If others are able to see your vision and that you are passionate about it, many will want to join you for the journey and the path to success. But your vision must also be specific and concrete enough to resist the challenges of naysayers. You'll always have your critics.

ENLARGE YOUR VISION

Yes, let's talk about enlarging your vision, even before you've fulfilled the original vision. Ephesians 3:20 reads: "*Now to him who is able to do immeasurably more than all we ask or imagine, according to his power that is at work within us."* God wants you to think big! He wants you to imagine big! In other words, God has blessings in store for you beyond what you can even think or imagine. That's awesome! So how do you tap into something that you can't see or even imagine exists?

First, you must have faith that God is true to His Word. Faith enables you to fight off the doubt that Satan uses against your mind to cause you to second guess yourself when you step out or are presented with something new or different from what you are accustomed to. In Ephesians 6: "Above all, put on the shield of faith, with which you will be able to quench all the fiery darts of the evil one." God's Word prepares you for what the enemy will be throwing at you so you will also be prepared to hold on to the future blessings that will come as a result of your faithfulness.

Second, you have to ask God to show you things you did not see before, understand things you did not understand before, and the courage to do things you have not done before. To enlarge your vision requires gaining wisdom and understanding. Where does wisdom and understanding come from? It comes from God. Proverbs 2:1–11 (NKJV) says:

> *So that you incline your ear to wisdom, And apply your heart to understanding; Yes, if you cry out for discernment, And lift up your voice for understanding, If you seek her as silver, And search for her as for hidden treasures; Then you will understand*

the fear of the LORD, *And find the knowledge of God. For the* LORD *gives wisdom; From His mouth comes knowledge and understanding; He stores up sound wisdom for the upright; He is a shield to those who walk uprightly; He guards the paths of justice, And preserves the way of His saints. Then you will understand righteousness and justice, Equity and every good path. When wisdom enters your heart, And knowledge is pleasant to your soul, Discretion will preserve you; Understanding will keep you.*

Third, pray and ask God to enlarge your vision or as Jabez called it, to enlarge your "territory," as is found in 1 Chronicles 4:10: "*Jabez cried out to the God of Israel, 'Oh, that you would bless me and enlarge my territory! Let your hand be with me, and keep me from harm so that I will be free from pain.' And God granted his request.*" The sad part for most of us is that we rarely tap into even a fraction of the blessings that God has in store for us. We should be filled with excitement every single day in knowing that the God we serve and pray to is the same awesome and only true God who hung the stars, breathed life into our bodies, makes the grass grow, who "clothes us in our right minds" daily, and provides for the birds and every living creature. He is the same God who raised Jesus Christ from the dead and that same power lives within each of us.[26] In order to receive from God, those things beyond what we can "think or imagine," all we are required to do is believe and follow His precepts.

POWER POINTS

- God's purpose for you is revealed through the vision He places in your heart.
- Spend time with God to receive your vision.
- God gives you specific gifts to fulfill His purpose for you.
- The two most important days in your life are the day you were born and the day you know why.
- You must always be willing to learn as a part of implementing your vision.
- Your vision must be clear and specific. Write it down.
- You must be able to communicate your vision to others.
- Your vision must motivate others to join you.
- Your vision must be strong enough to resist discouragement and naysayers.
- Stay connected to the source of the vision.
- Use vision like a "sixth sense" to guide you.
- Enlarge your vision.

Chapter 2

SET GOALS AND MAKE PLANS

And the LORD answered me, and said, "Write the vision, and make it plain upon tables, that he may run who reads it. For the vision is yet for an appointed time, but at the end it shall speak, and not lie: though it tarry, wait for it; because it will surely come, it will not tarry." Habakkuk 2:2–3 (NKJV)

SECRET #2: SUCCESSFUL ENTREPRENERURS MAKE PLANS AND SET GOALS

Successful people set goals and make plans. They plan their work and they work their plan.

If you live in the U.S. and were going to drive to Canada, but had never been there before, what's the first thing you would do? The answer is get a map. Well, today, you would plug the location into a GPS unit. The point is you can't drive to Canada without planning for the trip and having directions on how to get there.

The same is true for success in business. You can't get to where you want to go if you don't know where you are going or how you are going to get there. Successful people first set goals, based on the vision of where they want to go, then develop a plan to reach those goals. Yet, in order to become successful at setting meaningful goals and developing plans, you must get in the habit of seeking God's wisdom and guidance through prayer first. His Word tells us, *"Do not be anxious about anything, but in every situation, by prayer and petition, with thanksgiving, present your requests to God."*[27] The wisdom you receive from God will protect and guide the plans you establish.[28] Setting specific measurable goals directs your focus, efforts, and energy on the attainment of those goals. Habakkuk 2:3 also provides instruction for exercising patience in the execution of the plans He places in us. The promise, however, is that the plans He has will lend the promised results in His time.

Before setting your business goals, it is vitally important to set goals for your personal life. What kind of income and lifestyle would you like to have? What are the things that are important in your life? What are your values? What are you passionate about? Spend time brainstorming and thinking through the core areas of your life, such as your role as a father, mother, husband, wife, friend, employee, ministry leader, entrepreneur. Imagine what you would like to see happen in those areas. List goals relating to your finances, career, physical health, church life, and other important areas of your life. Write them out on a separate sheet of paper. Start with developing an overall personal mission statement that will serve as a guide by which to measure whether the actions you take are moving you toward the goals you set. Your personal mission statement should state your purpose is in life. Next write out where you want to be:

- a year from now
- three years from now
- five years from now
- ten years from now.

NO BOUNDARIES

Don't sell yourself short when setting your goals. Your goals come from your dreams so don't limit your dreams. Dream big! When you limit dreams, you limit your goals and subconsciously place boundaries and barriers to achieving things God has already made you good at. Dream boldly! No one is going to punish you for dreaming and setting goals beyond where they think you should. Here's a secret: It's OK, these are *your goals*. There is no reason to limit yourself in setting them. If you are worried about what others will think of you, skip over to Chapter 3 on Courage, read it then come back. Let's not waste any more time not fully exploring the corners of your mind, utilizing the your gift of *imagination* to see where this leads you. It's a wonderful gift. Dust it off and use it! Push yourself to think beyond ordinary, mediocre and routine expectations that may have been shaped by your past. God wants you to try Him[29].

God is ready to use you to do extraordinary things – just as He used ordinary people like Moses and a young David to do great things.[30] Don't put yourself in a box. More importantly, don't put God in a box. I often tell myself that God gave me the same twenty-four hours in a day that He gave Oprah. Also, I say that I put my pants on the same way as Bill Gates, one leg at a time. It's about how you use and manage the time God has given you. Understand and know that God has great things in store for you. The reason you will be able to do these great things is because it is God's power within you that is at work.[31] Goal setting is the time where the seeds of what is possible for you and your business begins to sprout and take shape to be increased by God in amazing ways.[32] Using your gift of imagination is the first step to bringing into fruition what God has given you the ability to accomplish. Guess what? Everything around you was once a thought that ultimately became a reality. Referenced in the Introduction, this scripture bears repeating. In Romans 4:17 (NKJV) God's Word shows us how to use our imagination and how it works when He gave Abraham the promise or covenant. It says:

> *As it is written, "I have made you a father of many nations" in the presence of Him whom he believed – God, who gives life to the dead and <u>calls those things which do not exist as though they did.</u>"*

Abraham had to imagine and envision what that promise looked like. He believed and had faith in God that the promise would become a reality. With faith as your anchor, you have to call those things that do not exist as though they do exist. You are calling things and promises of God from the spiritual realm and bringing them into the physical realm where you can take action on them. There is absolutely no reason you cannot imagine yourself being a prosperous individual or highly successful, healthy, and happy businessperson. Have the influences of the world and what others might think gotten you so uptight that you won't even imagine that you can be in a better place than you are now? Surely not!

Take a moment right now to imagine if you had all the money in the world and could do whatever you desired, what would that *feel* like? Resist the influences telling you not to go there, but go there anyway and get into the moment. This is the beginning of charting the course for your success. What does it *feel* like if ten years from now you could say you achieved all the goals and success you desired? What does it *feel* like to have all the energy you need to accomplish your goals? What does it *feel* like to be or accomplish whatever it is you desire for yourself? Write down and describe, in a short paragraph what it *feels* like to be the person you imagine you can be. Call this your personal "reality statement." Read it to yourself every night until you memorize it. Block out all the challenges of the day, meditate on what your success *feels* like and allow God to instruct your conscious and subconscious mind. Job 33:15-16 (NKJV) says: *"In a dream, in a vision of the night, when deep sleep falls upon men, While slumbering on their beds; then He opens the ears of men, and seals their instruction."* Doing this exercise every night prepares you for the next day and the actions you must take to move toward your goals and ultimate success. (Also see, Joshua 1:8-9 (NIV) As a part of your nightly prayer, include your reality statement, reading it aloud and asking God for His favor on your life and your vision. Each morning when you awake, spend time with God in prayer or meditation and again include your reality statement. It's truly amazing what this powerful exercise will do for you. It was during the night when God appeared to Solomon and said to him, *"Ask for whatever you want me to give you."*[33] We know that Solomon did not ask for riches or personal wealth. He asked God to give him wisdom and knowledge to lead God's people. God not only gave Solomon wisdom and knowledge, He gave him wealth, possessions and honor no other king has ever possessed. That same favor is available to each of us to propel us in reaching our goals.

Getting back to setting specific goals, be certain to include things you are passionate about and things that give your life purpose and meaning. List things close to your heart. What are your values and aspirations? There is no greater inner peace you can have than when the goals for your personal life are consistent, blended, and meshed with the goals for what you do in business. That's the reason for setting goals in your personal life first. Now you're ready to plan and write down goals for your business.

SETTING GOALS AND PLANS FOR YOUR BUSINESS

When it comes to successful planning and executing a plan, one of the most inspirational stories in the Bible, can be found in the book of Nehemiah. Nehemiah was thought of as having the impossible goal of leading his people to rebuild the Wall of Jerusalem.

After acknowledging his goal, the first thing Nehemiah did was to pray to God for the success of his plan to rebuild the Wall.

> *Lord, let your ear be attentive to the prayer of this your servant and to the prayer of your servants who delight in revering your name. Give your servant success today by granting him favor in the presence of this man. I was cupbearer to the king.* (Nehemiah 1:11, NIV)

After many trials, Nehemiah was ultimately successful in reaching his God-inspired goal of rebuilding the Wall of Jerusalem.[34] Just like Nehemiah, in business, you must *plan your work* and *work your plan*. For those just starting out or even if you have been in business for a while, your plans and goals should include some of the following:

- The type of legal structure for your business. Corporation, limited-liability company, Sub-Chapter S-corporation, partnership, limited partnership or sole proprietorship.
- The type of product or service you will offer. (This often manifests itself through your gifts, talents, or things you are good at or for which you have a passion.)
- How much money you plan to make in your business.
- Develop a realistic budget
- How many employees you anticipate will work for you.
- The markets you plan to serve.

- Meeting the key people who may be able to help you along the way. (Pray for God's favor with these people.)
- The things you will do to gain a competitive advantage over your competition.
- The level of financing you will need.
- The type of niche you can identify and serve where customers will demand your products or services.

Don't confuse goal setting with developing a specific business plan that involves the nuts and bolts of setting up and running a business. They are different and done at different phases of planning.

The goal-setting phase, which is a part of the strategic planning process, is the time to dream big and *think* outside the proverbial box. To be successful in business, you will soon learn that you will often operate outside the box to respond to challenges that come your way.

As you develop and write down your goals, an amazing thing occurs. A plan of action for how you will actually attain these goals begins to come into focus. Your creativity and energy combine to form a synergy that creates a roadmap for your next steps. These steps will set you on the path to achieving the goals you have set. What happens is that the seeds that have been planted in you are beginning to take root. The key, however, is to get the plan and vision out of your head and onto paper or into your computer. This is the first act to bringing your goal into reality. If your goal is to be a millionaire or financially independent in five years, envision the dollar amount and write it down. (By the way, I'm available for lunch when you reach it.) Your goal may be to have a chain of restaurants in five years or to open a specialty shop next year. Your goal may be to eliminate some debt before starting your business. In that case, for example, list all of your debt, write down a time frame for eliminating it, then develop a plan that includes how much money you will apply to eliminate the specific debt you target. We'll talk more about debt later.

PLANNNG IS FUNDAMENTAL

One of the biggest reasons for the failure of many small businesses is the owners don't believe they need to set goals or do planning. If you don't plan and set goals, the vision and energy you need to guide and grow your business will never take shape and come to fruition. Benjamin Franklin once said that by failing to prepare, you are preparing to fail. In other words, if you fail to plan, it goes without saying, you plan to fail.

Establishing plans is God's way of allowing you to act on those things in the present that you can control; and to reach, in the future, the goals you have set. Making plans and setting goals is not a haphazard process. It's not one where you simply pray and then hope that God will "make it all right" when you have not done what God requires of you. Luke 14:28 says: *"Suppose one of you wants to build a tower. Won't you first sit down and estimate the cost to see if you have enough money to complete it?"* As a part of planning, you must set forth, evaluate, and make preparations to act on those things that will lead to attaining the goals you have set.

Planning and setting goals is an intentional and precise process. However, a major factor to understand on your road to success is how those plans can change. Your goals may change only slightly, but your plans are a work-in-progress and can change for any number of reasons. Plans can change because you become more knowledgeable or discover a better way to accomplish a task. They can change because of new trends in the market place. They can change because of distractions that arise in your business or personal life. They change because of competition. The point is not to be so rigidly tied to the plans you make that you lose sight of your goal, for the sake of saying you did it your own way.

After you have written the goals for your business, I recommend an exercise to refine them. You can do that through a process called setting "S.M.A.R.T." goals.[35] Refining your goals through this process will make them become razor sharp and help avoid the frustration that comes from drifting or confusion as to whether you are still on the right path. It's a short and sweet exercise that can give you real benchmarks to track your progress. (Please note that it is important to first set your goals *without* reference to the S.M.A.R.T. process. This will help you avoid being inhibited in your thinking, or trying to fit a goal into the S.M.A.R.T. format before you have decided what the overall goal is.)

Goals should be Specific, Measurable, Attainable, Relevant, and Time bound.

- **S – Strategic and Specific**

  A goal should identify a specific action or event that will take place. It answers the questions: Who? and What?

- **M – Measurable**

  A goal needs to be measurable so you can determine that the results or outcome expected have been achieved. It answers the question: How?

- **A – Attainable**

  A goal should challenge people to do their best, but a goal also needs to be achievable.

- **R – Relevant**

  Goals need to pertain directly to the performance challenge being managed.

- **T – Time Bound**

  Enough time needs to be allowed to achieve a goal. But not too much time, which can affect project performance. It answers the question: When?

DEVELOP A STRATEGIC PLAN

As the chief executive officer of your company, you are the leader who must marshal all the resources and people necessary to successfully operate your business profitably. The most efficient way to do that is to develop a strategic plan. Sure you can dismiss the notion that you should consider yourself as the CEO of your small business. You can even ignore the need to have a strategic plan. But just like a pilot trying to fly a plane at night without instruments, you greatly decrease the chances you will reach your desired destination. A strategic plan can help save you time, money, and sleepless nights. Developing a well-thought-out strategic plan can be an inspirational and foundational tool to chart the path to success. In addition, a strategic plan gives you a high-level view of your path to success as well as ground-level strategies for reaching each goal. Your strategic plan establishes measurable goals, objectives, tasks and benchmarks that keeps everyone involved accountable to the mission. It also identifies the people, processes, systems and resources necessary to successfully accomplish each goal. When you get off course, your strategic plan is there to put you back on course. If your goals change, your strategic plan can be modified so that all members of the team will be aware of the change and everyone continues to work in unison toward the desired goals. The small business that develops and adheres to a strategic plan that includes a marketing plan that outlines how to generate leads and convert those leads to sales is greatly enhancing its chances for success in a highly competitive and challenging marketplace.

While some companies do strategic planning over the course of several days, a small business can develop a basic strategic plan in as few as three to four hours. Because of the importance a strategic plan can play in your success, I recommend setting aside at least six to eight hours, particularly for an ongoing small business. A strategic plan helps you refine the processes by which you reach the goals that have been set. I break strategic planning down into two phases. Phase I, Preliminary Planning, and Phase II, Strategic Plan Development.

PHASE I. Preliminary Planning

Step 1. Develop a mission statement. A mission statement is needed to set out the purpose and overall direction for your business. The goals you set should be aligned with the mission of your business and further the mission.

Step 2. Perform a SWOT analysis. This is an exercise whereby you assess and evaluate the capabilities of your business. As a small-business owner, it is important for you to have a realistic assessment of the current standing of your business in relation to your goals. Performing such an assessment is a simple process and should be done whether you are already in business or thinking about starting a business. In other words, you must answer the question, what are the **s**trengths and **w**eaknesses of what you currently have. This will assist you in reaching the goals you have set. What are your greatest **o**pportunities and **t**hreats? Going through this exercise will give you clarity about where your business is deficient or strong. One of the best tools I have found in assessing a business's current standing (and future opportunities) is to conduct a SWOT analysis. Often used by large companies, it is equally effective for small businesses. As described above you list your business's individual *strengths, weaknesses, opportunities* and *threats*.[36] Get a sample of a SWOT analysis, a strategic-plan template and a sample mission statement on my website. http://receiveandachievenow.com/chapter2

PHASE II. Strategic Plan Development

Step 1. Outline Status of Business. Once you have completed the SWOT analysis, you will need to rank and analyze each of the four categories to formulate goals and objectives based on what you seek to accomplish in your business. The result here is you will have a realistic assessment of where you stand in relation to fulfilling the mission statement you've developed. In this step, you simply list things as they currently are in your business. For example, "Current form of business is a sole proprietorship." If one of your goals is for your business to become a limited liability company (LLC), you list that as a goal.

Step 2. Set Goals. We talked a lot previously about setting goals. Review the recommended strategies in this chapter. Goals should enable you to fulfill your mission statement. As stated in Step 1, if the goal is to "become a limited-liability company by November 30," list that under the section for goals. Examples of other goals: "Hire HR director by September 20;" or "Increase revenue by 25 percent in next quarter."

Step 3. Action Steps. Step 3 is where the rubber meets the road. Here you list the action steps that must be performed to enable you to reach the goals you have set. These action steps are the movement and specific tasks to bridge the gap between Step 1, where you currently stand, and Step 2, your goal. These are actions that propel your business to the next level. For example, under this section list: (1) "Get two quotes from online to become an LLC;" (2) "Engage lowest cost vendor to file LLC papers by November 15 – Task assigned to Tom." Other examples: Set up mobile website by Sept. 15 – Tracey;" "Hire office manager by November 20 – Debbie;" "Update and e-mail customer survey with each point of sale for the fourth quarter – Jason." Notice that a name and a deadline date is always assigned to an action step.

Step 4. Develop an "Anti-Mire Action Plan" (A-MAP) [37]

This next step is one I've introduced in the strategic planning process for small businesses. Performing this exercise can be such a game-changing multiplier for enabling you to manage distractions and remain on track for accomplishing your goals. I want you to follow me as I introduce it with this odd question:

> *"What plans do you have to deal with the things that get in the way of the plans you have?"*

The answer to this question can be found in Psalms 40:2 which says:

He lifted me out of the slimy pit, out of the mud and mire; he set my feet on a rock and gave me a firm place to stand.

In life there will be challenges and temptations that weigh heavily on your soul and will impede your efforts to get closer to God. But fortunately God always provides a way out that gets you back on track and focused once again on Him. (1 Corinthians 10:13) The same is true in business in that you need a plan to deal with all the distractions, challenges and problems that get in your way and prevent you from reaching goals or executing on your overall strategic plan. You need a plan to put your feet on solid rock with a place to stand so you can confidently move forward to reaching your goals, and getting there in the time you establish. The best way to do that is to develop an Anti-Mire Action Plan or A-MAP. Developing an Anti-Mire Action Plan is the process of reviewing and listing those practical and unanticipated things that are a part of your daily life or business that could delay, hinder, or prevent you from accomplishing the Action Steps and Goals in your strategic plan. Webster defines *mire* as (a) "heavy, often deep sludge or slush;" (b) something "to hamper or hold back;" (c) a troublesome or interactive situation." That's what we do in developing an Anti-Mire Action Plan. It gives you the ability to anticipate or look ahead at the things that hamper, hold you back, or may be troublesome on your journey to success and reaching your goals. The A-MAP reveals blind spots that can result in high levels of frustration and disillusionment for aspiring and seasoned entrepreneurs. Here are some examples of things you may see on a small-business Anti-Mire Action Plan.

1. Payments on personal debt are draining funds for business operations. Need to reduce the debt first.
2. My aging parents are requiring more attention. Need to stabilize how I care for them.
3. Short on financial resources and credit is poor. A professional or personal relationship that has you distracted
4. Football season is approaching.
5. I'm being given more responsibility on the job. Don't have time to start my new business.
6. Constant interruptions, meetings, e-mails, and the telephone each day devour my time.
7. I have to care for a sick child or spouse.
8. Must take my daughter to soccer practice and my son to baseball practice.
9. Two children in college that don't have scholarships.

In other words, things on this list include practical things we tend to overlook or ignore when setting goals. The Anti-Mire Action Plan keeps in front of you real, but practical things in life relating to your time, finances, relationships, and health that affect the timing of the accomplishment of the Action Steps and Goals you have set. Because life happens, I don't want you to give up on your goals and dreams because they may not have occurred in the time you set. You simply need to know that life does happen, even when you make plans and set goals. But here, as much as any place you must not fall prey to the victims' mentality. You must trust in the Lord and acknowledge Him and He will direct your path. It's about staying focused, managing these things, and being prepared.

Step 5. Weekly Progress Review. Review your progress weekly to update and check off the Action Steps you've completed. If you are a small business with few employees and need additional capacity to get some of the work done, consider getting a relative or friend to assist. Also, outsourcing has become affordable for small businesses. The evolution of technology and the Internet have made outsourcing an extremely affordable tool for small-business owners. Virtual assistants (VA) have become indispensible for many small-business owners and perform their services from numerous locations in the U.S., and around the globe. Of course, like everything else, you need to shop around and do your homework before hiring a VA. One of the biggest advantages is you don't have the ongoing payroll overhead expense of an employee. Depending on your type of business, some VAs will be better suited than others to assist you. Some will even give you a trial run before you are required to pay them. A VA can be a solo business owner or a large company that employs thousands. Two countries that have embraced this form of outsourcing are India and the Philippines. The CEO of a VA company I've considered using, says to reduce the chance of having a bad experience, you should always use a company that has at least one office located in the U.S., India, or Europe because the laws for protecting your rights are stronger and more mature in this area.

Step 6. Identify your niche. Finally, developing a niche is critically important for the success of your business and should always be a key part of strategic planning for your business. It should be factored in as a part of all five steps of your strategic plan. Many small-business owners are doomed to failure because they never grasp the concept that they cannot be everything to everyone. An all too often overlooked strategy for small-business owners is to have or develop a niche that fills a strong need for your customers and clients. You must have something that sets you apart from the competition. You want your marketing message to resonate and dominate with your potential customers and clients. Ask yourself these questions in developing and fine tuning your niche: 1) Are customers actively looking for your product? 2) Is your product or service difficult to obtain from other sources? 3) Why would customers buy from you as compared to your competitor? 4) What solution does your product or service solve for the customer? What advantage will the customer enjoy in buying your product over your competitor? What "pain" does your product or service relieve for your customer? Will your customers feel they are better off in purchasing your product?

POWER POINTS

- Set goals and plans.
- Seek God's wisdom for guidance.
- Understand that plans must be flexible to change.
- Set goals for your personal life, then your business.
- Don't limit yourself based on the past.
- Don't limit God in setting your goals.
- Do not worry about what others think.
- Use your gift of imagination. Call those things which do not exist as though they do exist.
- Envision what success looks like. Imagine what success feels like (see it – feel it).
- Set S.M.A.R.T. goals.
- Develop a strategic plan.
- Develop a niche. Fill a strong need.
- Learn about and use virtual assistants.

PART III.
THE STRENGTH TO MOVE FORWARD

Challenges in my life are opportunities for me to be strengthened and move closer to God. I will carry my challenges and burdens to Him in prayer and leave them there. I will not let fear, guilt, pride, sorrow or self-pity paralyze me to inaction. God did not give me a spirit of fear. Each obstacle I overcome will be a testament of God's goodness, His faithfulness and His grace. I will persistently press toward my goals because I know that He is always with me and there to comfort me.

Reference:
James 1:2-3 (NIV)
Matthew 11:28–30 (NIV)
2 Timothy 1:7, NKJV
Philippians 3:14
Psalm 23 (NIV)

Chapter 3

COURAGE

For God has not given us a spirit of fear, but of power and of love and of a sound mind.

2 Timothy 1:7 NKJV

SECRET #5: SUCCESSFUL ENTREPRENEURS HAVE COURAGE

Entrepreneurs are seldom thought of as courageous, a little daring perhaps, but not courageous. But to be a success in business, you must have courage. Courage is taking action in the face of fear. Fear one of Satan's greatest and most effective tools. To effectively deal with fear, you must be willing to step out and take action when circumstances and people around you (naysayers) are providing you all the reasons you can't be successful as an entrepreneur. Circumstances can include not only external factors, but your inner fears and beliefs you must deal with. One of the quickest ways to get on a path to success is dealing with the fear of what others think about you. These are the naysayers and most often, they are people who are closest to you. Recognizing first this is a barrier, then exercising courage to break through it will be a major accomplishment feeling the freedom to move in to a new and exciting space in your life. Avoid and ignore naysayers when you can, but in your mind, "flip the script". Let their negative attitudes be a source of motivation for to take action and be a success. Rise above the level of their thinking by praying for them and watch how God will move in your life. Fear of being ridiculed has kept many good people out of business who would otherwise have become successful entrepreneurs.

Running a business is not for the faint of heart. For there are indeed many pitfalls out there. Of the many small-business owners I've talked with or helped, the fear comes primarily from the unknown. That includes fear of not knowing where to turn for information; fear of not knowing if you have what it takes to run a business; fear of not knowing how to plan; fear of not knowing how to market or sell; fear of not being able to pay your bills. As a consequence, too many who do have what it takes to succeed focus on the fear of failure. Because God did not give you a spirit of fear, you must overcome this fear of failure, or you will never take the first step to change your circumstance. Start by moving your focus from the potential for failure to the God-given opportunity for success and a life filled with joy and abundance. This mental redirection of what you focus on will immediately free you of the heavy burden of self-doubt and inadequacy that fear places on your back. You break the chains with the adjustment. Take a moment to feel the new found sense of freedom.

Your success comes when you step out and move forward in spite of the fear. Don't live your life wondering what might have been if only you had taken that first step. Each step gets easier and the path becomes clearer the more you look to the True Source for the strength and courage to forge ahead in the face of your fears.

Fear and the pressure it generates can paralyze you into inaction. But God has given you all the courage and confidence you need to face challenges or difficult decisions you must make. Fear affects people differently. It can have a debilitating effect on your personal life as well as affect your decision to even go into business. Fear can definitely affect the way you handle obstacles in business, but the shift of your focus from the thing you fear to a focus on God's Word will have an immediate positive impact on your confidence in conquering that fear.

CONQUERING FEAR

In business as in life, it's important to understand the effect fear can have on you. Pastor Charles Stanley explains the detrimental effects of fear this way:[38]

- Fear causes confusion. A fearful person will have a difficult time thinking clearly.
- Fear contributes to indecision. When someone is afraid of making a mistake, he or she often delays making any choice at all.

- Fear hinders us from accomplishing God's will. An apprehensive person misses opportunities because he or she expects failure.
- Fear damages self-confidence. Frightened people can seem insecure and incompetent because they doubt their ability to succeed.
- Fear affects our relationships.
- Fear can lead to full-blown panic.
- Fear sometimes makes us believe we cannot handle things when in reality we can. We just have to believe in God's Word and step out in faith.
- Fear can cause us to turn to bad habits that affect our health and well-being.

An important step to addressing fear is to have a self-awareness that it is fear we are dealing with. This is not necessarily easy to do once fear has engulfed you. Fear causes anxiety and can prevent you from resting at night and hinder your obedience to God. The big challenge is how to overcome fear, become courageous, face your fears, and conquer them.

In a sermon he preached years ago, Minister Chuck Harris, a good friend, recommended dealing with fear by using the three "C's". 1) Confront it; 2) Control it; and, 3) Conquer it.

1.)   Confront it!

The absolute key to a life of success and abundance is to first recognize what it is that really holding you back. Ask yourself, why is it that I have not already achieved the type of life I truly desire? What is it that I really fear? Is it fear of not being able to pay my bills? Is it that I don't feel I'm good enough to run a business, or take my business to the next level? Am I worried about what people will think of me? Whatever the fear, you must call it out and confront it. As you identify your fear, you confront it by first calling to mind and reading aloud God's Word: *The LORD is my light and my salvation; whom shall I fear? The LORD is the strength of my life; of whom shall I be afraid.* (Psalm 27:1)

You serve a God of abundance, so get rid of that fearful mindset of scarcity and lack. Confront it and stop worrying about not having enough. Focus on the Word of God and how amazing He truly is in supplying all your needs. God has equipped you with gifts to manifest abundance, if you trust and believe in Him. Don't be like the servant who, as Jesus taught in Matthew 25:14-30, took the one talent his master gave him and buried it in the ground rather than invest it because he was filled with so much fear. You want to be like the two servants in the parable, who the master gave two and five talents, respectively. They both took action and doubled their talents which greatly pleased the master, who said to them, *"Well done, good and faithful servant! You have been faithful with a few things; I will put you in charge of many things."* The servant who buried his talent in the ground never confronted his fear. As a result, he allowed fear to paralyze him into inaction. The master even took the one talent the servant had and gave it to one of the servants who had doubled his talents. Don't wait another day. Confront your fear! Call it out! It is your first step to freedom and a life of abundance.

2) Control it!

Once you have honestly identified the fear and called it out, it is important now to control it. Controlling your fear is essential because it's easy to go back to old habits or a place of complacency that is inside your comfort zone where you are ineffective and living a life of timidity rather than a boldness and abundance. But again, for each area of fear, call upon the Word. *"For God has not given us a spirit of fear, but of power and of love and of a sound mind (2 Timothy 1:7, NKJV).* Because controlling your fear is such a difficult place in that it requires a daily, long-term commitment, it is vital to remember you are never alone in your struggles as God tells you in Isaiah 41:13 (NIV), *"For I am the LORD your God who takes hold of your right hand and says to you, Do not fear, I will help you."* Just like a child, whose hand you would hold in a big crowd or in a strange place, your Heavenly Father holds your hand, gives you comfort and protection from whatever challenge you face. Understand that God specializes in taking fearful broken vessels and turning them into fruitful centers of influence.

3) Conquer it!

The final step in overcoming fear is to conquer it. Once you've successfully trekked through the challenge of confronting your fears then controlling them daily, I have good news for you. Satan and the tool of fear he uses to immobilize you have already been defeated. So by being in Christ and holding God's hand as you control your fears, you are walking in victory over Satan and all your fears. (Revelation 12:10-12 (MSG). You must, however, put on your shield of faith daily and allow God to give you 24/7 protection from all the fiery darts Satan will continue to throw at you.[39] James 4:7 says: "Submit yourselves, then, to God. Resist the devil, and he will flee from you.

Finally, confirmation that you have conquered your fears comes when you can move forward with a sense of joy and peace in the face of fears He says: *"Consider it pure joy, my brothers and sisters, whenever you face trials of many kinds, because you know that the testing of your faith produces perseverance"* (James 1:2–3, NIV). Who else but Christ can give you peace when fear seeks to engulf you? No one! That's because this is not just any peace. This is the peace of God which is like no other: *"Peace I leave with you, My peace I give to you; not as the world gives do I give to you. Let not your heart be troubled, neither let it be afraid"* (John 14:27–28).

The real secret to confronting, controlling and conquering your fears is follow the example set by Jesus Christ when Christ was in the wilderness for 40 days and had to deal with the temptations placed before Him by Satan. Each time Christ was tempted, He referred to the Word of God in response to Satan. On every occasion Jesus preceded His response with these words: *"It is written..."*[40] So it is conquering your fear. The formula underlying the Three C's above points directly to God's Word and is as follows:

Step 1 – *Meditate on His Word.* (Confront it!)

> *My son, attend to my words; incline thine ear unto my sayings. Let them not depart from thine eyes;*

keep them in the midst of thine heart. For they are life unto those that find them, and health to all their flesh (Proverbs 4:20–22).

Step 2 – *Trust in His Word.* (Control it!)

Trust in the Lord with all your heart and lean not unto your own understanding. In all your ways, acknowledge him and He will direct your path (Proverbs 3:5–6).

Step 3 – *Step out on His Word.* (Conquer it!)

Be strong and courageous. Do not be afraid or terrified because of them, for the LORD your God goes with you; he will never leave you nor forsake you (Deuteronomy 31:6, NIV).

Stepping outside your comfort zone is necessary to grow in faith and trust, because only outside of your comfort zone will you be able to grow. It also helps to research, study and prepare. Do the research you need to do. Gather whatever facts you need to gather. Listen with your mind and heart. Know that whatever is outside your comfort zone, it is not too big for God to handle and carry you through. Memorize a favorite scripture and bring it to the forefront of your mind when you have a decision to make. Like an Olympic weightlifter, only by adding more weight beyond what has been lifted before will you get stronger and move toward winning that gold medal. The same principle applies to you. Be a person of action. Once you've made the first small step and exercised that small measure of faith, you will indeed grow and become stronger. The next steps become easier and easier.

The specific scripture that most often gives me courage and confidence is Romans 8:28, *"And we know that all things work together for good to those who love God, to those who are the called according to His purpose."* In other words, no matter what I face as I set out in business and other endeavors, I can have the confidence in knowing that God's favor is upon my plans and His purpose for my life will be fulfilled.

One of the most interesting things about fear I have observed in consulting with hundreds of small-business owners, is that the things they were most afraid of often never came to pass. A popular acronym that I have found useful in defining fear is **F**alse **E**vidence **A**ppearing **R**eal. Fear is a false purpose that can motivate us in a harmful direction.

You have gifts. Have the courage to use those gifts. Not only will you be blessed, you'll find that many others will be blessed along your road to great success.

POWER POINTS

- Courage is a necessary ingredient for success in business.
- God did not give you a spirit of fear.
- Don't let negative attitudes and naysayers cause you to not act or pursue your dreams.
- Understand that fear creates anxiety, can hinder your progress, and cause you to make bad decisions.
- Be realistic about confronting your fears.
- In the face of fear you must: Confront it, Control it and Conquer it.
- Conquer fear by meditating, trusting, and stepping out on God's Word.
- Know that God will never leave you nor forsake you.
- Practice operating outside your comfort zone.

Chapter 4

PERSEVERANCE

Therefore, since we are surrounded by such a great cloud of witnesses, let us throw off everything that hinders and the sin that so easily entangles. And let us run with perseverance the race marked out for us, fixing our eyes on Jesus, the pioneer and perfector of faith.

Hebrews 12:1–6 (NIV)

SECRET #3: PERSEVERANCE – THE QUIET STRENGTH WITHIN

Have you ever had to overcome a difficult situation in your life? Didn't it require you to reach deep within yourself to ultimately get through that situation? Were there times when you felt like giving up, but you hung in there to see it through? Friends, that's perseverance. *Perseverance* is defined as maintaining a steady, purposeful, and persistent course of action in spite of difficulties, obstacles, or discouragement.[41] Perseverance is the inner strength and determination that moves you forward in the face of a difficult situation. It is that trait that presses you onward when it seems the world is against you and obstacles are insurmountable. Put another way, perseverance is the increasing of your character by persistently overcoming obstacles using the gifts with which God has blessed you. God knows that our lives on this earth will be difficult and His Word tells us that. Nevertheless, we are called to seek His glory through it all because the trials and challenges make us stronger and the love He has poured in us empowers each of us to endure whatever comes. Consider Romans 5:1-5:

> *Not only so, but we also glory in our sufferings, because we know that suffering produces perseverance, perseverance, character; and character, hope. And hope does not put us to shame, because God's love has been poured out into our hearts through the Holy Spirit, who has been given to us.*

Universally, high achievers in business have stories to tell about perseverance. Glenn Farrington, whom I referenced in Chapter 1, once said to me in the early days of his business venture, "I don't even have money to buy diapers for my son, *but I can't quit now.*" Less than two years after that statement, we were well on our way to providing Internet service to 80 percent of the U.S. cruise-line industry. Glenn persevered through some very difficult times to get his product to market.

The rewards of owning and operating a business can be great. But gaining ultimate success will not be a cakewalk. There will be many obstacles. By understanding up front that obstacles and challenges are a normal part of the business landscape, you have uncovered one of the most potent secrets that high-performing entrepreneurs have in their arsenal. It's the knowledge that perseverance is required for success because it shapes their attitude and approach to dealing with the obstacles that routinely pop us on the path to great success.

ATTITUDE DETERMINES ALTITUDE

Dealing with challenges is largely a matter of having the right attitude. Your attitude toward handling obstacles and difficult situations has everything to do with your ultimate success in business and in life. If you become distraught at the first sign of an obstacle, you either have to change your attitude or find a different line of work where someone else calls the shots.

Successful people actually welcome challenges and obstacles because they know these things invite learning opportunities. More specifically, they know that obstacles are opportunities to grow and for God to shine through use the gifts He has provided. They already understand that they will become wiser and stronger once they go through the experience. If you are truly able to drill to the core of what *"attitude determines altitude"*, really, REALLY means, you will open the door of unlimited abundance for yourself and your business. It means that you have removed the limiting barriers, labels and circumstances the world has put on you. It means you are prepared to use your God-given gifts to tackle whatever obstacle comes and to have a Christ-like impact on those around you. It means that rejection or what people may think of you no longer concern you and you are able to step outside your comfort zone and grow. It means you don't fear stepping out to reach your goals despite not having all the details of how you will get there. It means you begin to understand that your journey is not about you, but about God's master plan, which includes filling you with joy to deal with challenges and obstacles each day. It means you are able to transition to the next difficult task and maintain a joyful attitude. Having the joy of the Lord is the key to maintaining an attitude that causes obstacles and rejection to roll off you like *"water off a ducks back."* It takes practice and trust in God to get there, but look at what God's Word says your attitude should be in how you should the face of challenges and trials. James 1:2-3 (NIV) says: *"Consider it pure joy, my brothers and sisters, whenever you face trials of many kinds, because you know that the testing of your faith produces perseverance. Let perseverance finish its work so that you may be mature and complete, not lacking anything."* Such an attitude, for most. is counter-intuitive. However, it is a game-changer. Through Christ, the joy He provides gives you the strength, confidence and endurance to handle any challenge. Like an athlete training for the Olympics, you must have endurance and be prepared for the obstacles that are surely to come.[42]

Having a positive attitude is more than just giving yourself an occasional pep talk or trying to keep yourself upbeat. There is no shortage of people, books, and online information available to tell you to keep your chin up, maintain a positive outlook, or to just "hang in there." Some of them may be useful, but the problem here is the source of the encouragement or the lack of an "everlasting" source. You can't have a positive attitude that will last if you are trying to do it in your own strength. You will eventually become tired, weak and discouraged. But Isaiah 40:28-29 (NIV) says: *"Do you not know? Have you not heard? The LORD is the everlasting God, the Creator of the ends of the earth. He will not grow tired or weary, and his understanding no one can fathom. He gives strength to the weary and increases the power of the weak."* Endurance to persevere to the success and abundance that awaits you can only come through the unchanging hand of God and persistent meditation on His Holy Word. Consider Joshua 1:8 (NIV) which says:

> *Keep this Book of the Law always on your lips; meditate on it day and night, so that you may be careful to do everything written in it. Then you will be prosperous and successful.*

It is the confidence in knowing that God's purpose will be fulfilled no matter how difficult or uncomfortable the obstacle is you face. Moreover, because Satan has already been defeated and we are believers in Jesus Christ, the battles we fight are from victory and not to victory.[43] That's why we can have joy, peace and the right attitude in the midst of storms and challenges. The storms are going to pass over and the challenges will be overcome. We will not only be stronger on the other side, we will be ready and much better prepared for the next challenge to come, whatever it is. Plus, the Christ-like attitude we exhibit in managing storms and challenges may be just the motivation others who are watching us need to move them one step closer to Christ.

THE ANGER FACTOR

There's one thing I need to add here about getting and maintaining the right attitude. If you are carrying anger or resentment against someone, you are going to have to let it go. I know you are probably saying to yourself, "I was on board with him up to this point." Now he's going to ask me to forgive John/Jane Doe for what they did to me and I can no longer be angry? No way! He does not know what they did to me!" You are correct. I don't know what they did to you, but it's not me asking you to forgive and let it go. It's what God's Word calls each of us to do:

> *Get rid of all bitterness, rage and anger, brawling and slander, along with every form of malice. Be kind and compassionate to one another, forgiving each other, just as in Christ God forgave you* (Ephesians 4:31, NIV).

Because Christ died on the cross for you and forgave your sins, in the face of rejection, you do have the capacity to forgive in any situation and you have the capacity to love in that very situation. 1 John 4:19 (NIV) says: "We love, because He first loved us."[44] The act of forgiveness is one of the most powerful tools God has given us to grow spiritually. When employed fully, it frees us from the chains of the past, cleanses and moves us closer to Him. It also brings about healing in ways we don't understand. In many situations, people with whom you are angry are not even aware you are carrying around anger against them. So who is your anger hurting? Often when a person is aware that you are angry with them, they will do little things to cause you even more aggravation and set you off. So the real question is, why give anyone that much control over <u>your</u> emotions? God's word instructs often to avoid and control anger. Proverbs 16:32 (NKJV) says: *"He who is slow to anger is better than the mighty, and he who rules his spirit than he who takes a city."*

The ability to control your anger is key to your success in business and enables you to avoid unnecessary encounters with unscrupulous individuals who have offended you. Such individuals can distract you from your goals and God's purpose for you. You have to identify the source of the anger, confront it, forgive, (not forget) release it and move on. You must be intentional about releasing anger. Anger left unchecked eats at you and in your mind gets worse. Proverbs 30:33 (NKJV) says:

> *For as churning cream produces butter, and as twisting the nose produces blood, so stirring up anger produces strife.*

It is only by taking on the qualities of Jesus Christ through the Holy Spirit that we can handle anger. Colossians 3:12 tells us, *"Therefore, as God's chosen people, holy and dearly loved, clothe yourselves with compassion, kindness, humility, gentleness and patience.* Seek godly counsel if you find that remnants of anger remain within you. Doing so is an acknowledgment that you want to have the right attitude and maintain the confidence that God will be there to carry you through whatever may come. When all else fails, look to what Christ endured and what He said for the benefit of all mankind as He hung on the cross. *"Father, forgive them, for they know not what they do."* Luke 23:34.

My mother, Verba's favorite scripture reading is the twenty-third Psalm. In verse four, you find these words: *"Yea, though I walk through the valley of the shadow of death, I will fear no evil; For You are with me. Your rod and Your staff, they comfort me."* You can have and maintain a positive attitude and hope in the future because God is constantly with you – protecting you. This knowledge enables you to persevere with the right attitude. There is nothing to fear. Here is Psalm 23 (NKJV) in its entirety:

> *The LORD is my shepherd; I shall not want. He makes me to lie down in green pastures; He leads me beside the still waters; He restores my soul; He leads me in the paths of righteousness, for His name's sake. Yea, though I walk through the valley of the shadow of death, I will fear no evil; For You are with me; You prepare a table before me in the presence of my enemies; You anoint my head with oil; My cup runs over. Surely goodness and mercy shall follow me, All the days of my life; And I will dwell in the house of the LORD, Forever.*

I have a cousin, Larry who is in construction and owns a drywall business. He attends church regularly and was usually very positive about most things. But Larry felt the only reason his business was thriving was because of his individual efforts in securing business. Certainly he believed his business could not survive if he were not there to personally work it. Recently Larry became despondent and depressed when he faced several personal challenges that included a divorce and having to serve jail time for six months for repeated traffic violations. On the day he surrendered to begin his time of incarceration, Larry's mind was filled with thoughts of losing his business and a new home he had recently purchased. He was certain he would have nothing to return to after he did his time. A few days into his term, he met an inmate who literally turned his life around. The inmate began to minister to him and read scripture to him daily. Larry also received frequent visits from his pastor, Nolan Branch. Soon Larry was ministering to other inmates and was given a trustee role in the kitchen. In the midst of all that he was going through, Larry's attitude had changed. He had decided to turn his circumstances over to God and serve God's purpose by spreading the Gospel while incarcerated. In his own words Larry said this:

"Once I turned my circumstances over to Jesus Christ and no longer worried about all the things that were on me, I felt more free than I have ever felt, even though I was locked up. God's Word gave me comfort and let me know that I would be OK even if I did not have a business or a home to go back to. I was in jail and my being there would serve His purpose. I thanked Him for the opportunity, even though it meant I had to go to jail to have my eyes opened. That's why

I am able to maintain a positive attitude and outlook. I can't describe the wonderful feeling of relief I felt in having those burdens lifted off me. I had to learn that it was about Him, not me. I was now free to minister not to just other inmates, but the guards and all who I came in contact with." Larry gave this advice: *"If you do what you should do by meditating on God's Word, He will surely do what He has promised to do in delivering you through!"* Larry did his six months; and during that time to his surprise, his mother Ann, stepfather Breely, and cousin Denzel, stepped in to operate his business and save his home from foreclosure. Larry continues to spread the Gospel at every turn and is developing a ministry to aid those who are incarcerated.

Martha Hawkins, a restaurant owner and friend in Montgomery, Alabama, is another person who epitomizes perseverance. Through much prayer, hard work, and perseverance, Martha lifted herself from living in public housing to becoming a restaurant owner and evangelist who is today renowned throughout the United States. This single mother of four, who suffered abuse as a child, including being raped, opened a restaurant nineteen years ago called *Martha's Place*.

Celebrities and people from all walks of life have frequented the restaurant for Martha's food and a chance to hear her story and the things she had to overcome. At her lowest point twenty years ago, Martha attempted suicide and was placed in a mental hospital. But despite these challenges, she began to read God's Word on a regular basis, Martha persevered and maintained her peace and joy through it all. It was from her low point that God gave her the vision and strength to open a restaurant and call it "Martha's Place." After 18 years in business, the economy and financial challenges forced her to close her doors. Martha knew, however, that this was not the end of her restaurant and with God's help, she would one day reopen. Martha boldly proclaims that: "When you persevere in Christ and one door is closed, be of good cheer, because God will surely open another for you.

During the time Martha's restaurant was closed, she continued spreading the Gospel of Jesus Christ while promoting her new book *Finding Martha's Place,* which was made possible by a caring internationally known corporate executive who had eaten at her restaurant each time he was in the Montgomery area. Martha never wavered in knowing that she would continue to find success as long as she had faith in God and continued to persevere. About 18 months after the doors to her restaurant were closed, Martha was approached by a local businessman who knew her and about her national reputation for serving great food. He wanted to partner with her. Martha knew it was God because she had no money to put in the restaurant. In March, 2012, the doors of Martha's Place restaurant reopened. She was in a new location and a new building, which she custom designed and business has been booming ever since the doors reopened. Martha says with great conviction, "It's just God and I give Him all the praise and glory for being God and faithful to His Word."

In business, bumps in the road come with the territory. The commitment to persevere is essential to give you the power not to become discouraged when you begin to hit those bumps. Often times these bumps come in waves and from several directions. Perhaps a key employee quits, or products for tomorrow's sale were not delivered, or cash for Friday's payroll will be short. But God's Word tells us to put on the shield of faith. With it, we can withstand

ALL the fiery darts of the wicked one.[45] As you overcome each obstacle, you gain more confidence and build stamina. Soon you will learn that there is no obstacle you cannot face with God's help.

The more difficult the obstacle, the more you'll grow in confidence and faith. You will become better prepared to press on toward the goals set before you.[46]

PREPARATION IS THE KEY

Being successful in business is like being successful in a war. If a soldier is in a war zone and unprepared for battle, he can easily be wounded or killed. The same holds true for business. If you are unaware that serious obstacles will come and are unprepared to address the obstacles, you will be defeated as well. You must prepare yourself to do business like a soldier preparing for war. High-performing athletes understand the importance of perseverance and live under its influence daily. No one knows this any better than Carnell "Cadillac" Williams, who in football at Auburn University, holds the #1 or #2 record in all-time stats in four separate categories that include: 1) rushing yards, 2) rushing attempts, 3) touchdowns, and 4) most "SEC Player of the Week" honors. In the category of "all-purpose yards," he ranks #3 of all-time for a single season. Behind Bo Jackson, many consider Cadillac to be one of the greatest running backs to play football at Auburn. In 2005, he was the National Football League's Rookie of the Year and the Associated Press's Offensive Player of the Year.[47]

Cadillac says that early on, his mother, Sherry, instilled in him the virtues of perseverance. He says, "My mom often told me that I could do anything I wanted to do, but it would not be easy. Obstacles will come up that will make it easy for you to quit, but if you want success, you are going to have to work through whatever roadblocks come your way." Cadillac added:

> *"It was my strong faith in God and prayers that helped prepare me because I've had to face some pretty big obstacles over the years. But I didn't look at them as obstacles. I saw them as opportunities. I had faith that God could deliver me through anything. God has given me a strong will to persevere and endure obstacles. I set the bar very high for myself, so there are always obstacles I must overcome and work through. My will and determination is often a topic of conversation among members of my family. When I suffered a couple of major injuries at Auburn, I knew the rehab would be difficult and take time. However, I never lost faith that I would come back strong. I stayed with the rehab program that was laid out for me and had a wonderful final year, with the support of my coaches and teammates, before leaving Auburn."*
>
> *"The same thing happened with the two knee injuries I suffered while with the Tampa Bay Buccaneers. They said no one in the history of the NFL had ever come back from injuries to both knees like I had. But I*

understood that to fulfill the goals I had set for myself for my NFL career, it would be necessary for me to persevere through surgeries, pain, and difficult rehab – and that's exactly what I did. Was it easy? Absolutely not. Achieving goals you set that are worthwhile is never easy. To be successful, you are going to have to work through challenges and obstacles of all kinds, including things that you can't anticipate.

To be among the best at what you do, your single focus can only be to press on, no matter how tough it gets. "Many people won't understand this, but working through the pain and obstacles is where you find the most success and the most joy. Sure, no one expected me to return to the field after two "career ending" injuries, but I chose not to believe what 'they said' and I persevered. I chose to believe that, 'I can do all things through Christ who strengthens me."

"During the 2011-12 season, I was grateful to be back on the field and felt good running the ball. 'What is impossible with man is possible with God.' I started a new chapter in St. Louis with the Rams. Every yard I gained was a testament that Jesus Christ is Lord and is faithful to His promises. God has blessed me in so many ways. I'm looking forward to embracing the challenges and the success which lie ahead for me.

Cadillac is a great young man and his life's story is quite inspirational. I told him I wanted to see his story in a book soon.

So how do you prepare to persevere in business? Utilize this four-point plan:

1) <u>Plan your work and work your plan</u>. Most small-business owners fail to understand that lack of planning adds to the burdens of operating a business. Effective planning helps you see into the future. It will keep down surprises and navigate the challenges ahead. Planning gives you more time to prepare to overcome the obstacles. Planning makes you more efficient. Every ten minutes you spend planning equates to an hour saved. Planning is a tool and process of looking ahead and preparing for what is to come. The Message version of Proverbs 21:5 says: *Careful planning puts you ahead in the long run; hurry and scurry puts you further behind*. Planning enables you to complete the tasks of each day and accomplish your overall objectives for achieving your goals much faster. Here's a secret: Planning is a simple process that gives you the opportunity to align your plans with what God has in store for you. It puts the supernatural forces of your Heavenly Father to work for you. Planning is not rocket science or something to avoid. If you want to make the journey to success easier and the load lighter, sit down and plan.

2) <u>View obstacles as an opportunity with an expectancy that you will overcome them</u>. This is a time for endurance and for you to exercise your gifts, talents, and ingenuity to subdue and prevail over the obstacle.

3) <u>Don't become tentative when a few challenges or obstacles come your way</u>. That generates fear and will impede forward progress. There is no room for fear, but when fear appears, that's the signal telling you it's time to forge ahead, knowing that Christ will never leave you or forsake you. Maintain a positive outlook; examine your options with a clear head; " keep your wits about you"; seek the wise counsel of others and call on God's mighty power within you to carry you through the challenge. If others have done it, so can you!

4) <u>Have an attitude of gratitude</u>. That is, be grateful and give thanks to God for all He has brought you through, and for the hedge of protection he has placed around your life and your family. He has placed you in a position to be a business owner, an entrepreneur – one who serves others in the marketplace. Especially in the marketplace should you be grateful for the favor and blessings you have received and those which will come your way as you venture out. This is one of the single most important things you can do for your spiritual and emotional state as you face the challenges of each day. An attitude of gratitude is like a sponge that soaks up all the daily dirt and grime you must deal with. Have a commitment to God's Word, a peaceful heart, a prayerful life and a concern for God's Will. An attitude of gratitude will follow.[48] 1 Thessalonians 5:18 says: *"In everything give thanks: for this is the will of God in Christ Jesus concerning you."*

POWER POINTS

- Understand that challenges will come. It's just life – you must press forward.
- Having the right attitude empowers you to deal with challenges effectively.
- Understand that with Christ as your source, God's purpose will be served and you can have victory over any challenge that comes your way.
- Plan your work and work your plan.
- View obstacles as an opportunity to exercise the gifts God has given you.
- Attitude determines altitude.
- Maintain an attitude of gratitude.
- Call on God's mighty power within you. It will strengthen you and eliminate fear.

Chapter 5

PASSION

Never be lacking in zeal, but keep your spiritual fervor, serving the Lord. Romans 12:11 (NIV)

SECRET #4: SUCCESSFUL ENTREPRENEURS HAVE PASSION

P assion is the energy needed to drive you to do the things you must do to make your business a success. If you do not feel passionate about your business, or business idea, you should find something else to do. No person who has ever attained any level of success has done it without passion and being passionate about their vision for their business or personal life. Three key elements of igniting your passion are to first, find something that you enjoy doing, second, it must be something that you are good at or have the ability to excel in, and third, it must be linked to something you care about. (See discussion on Self-Motivation, p. 60). Passion is also infectious. When others see that you are passionate about what you are doing, that passion spreads to them as well.

Passion is the engine that keeps your feet running when you are tired. It gets you up on those cold mornings to do the things necessary to fulfill your goals. Passion will keep you going on those days when you wonder why you started down this path in the first place. It will keep you moving when things get difficult. Passion is the fire within you, and you want to make certain that fire never goes out. Follow your passion and let it give you the drive you need each and every day. Passion will move you even when other urges want to go in a different direction.

THE FIRE WITHIN

Passion comes from the heart. It is the fire that moves you to take action every single day. Passion propels and compels you to act. Consider the two travelers to whom Jesus appeared and spoke to after His resurrection while they were traveling on a road to a city just outside of Jerusalem. They acknowledged passion for His teachings after Jesus disappeared from their sight: *"They said one to another, 'Weren't our hearts burning within us, while he spoke to us along the way, and while he opened the Scriptures to us?'"*[49] In business you need to constantly feel that same "burning within," which will move you to action.

Despite his determination to stop even talking about the things God placed on his heart, the prophet Jeremiah soon learned that his passion for God's Word became so strong, he declared that it was, in effect, useless for him to try and contain his love for God's Word. Clearly, Jeremiah was *fired up* for God's Word. But that's what passion does. It fires you up. You cannot be mediocre or indecisive and find the success and prosperity God has promised. Revelation 3:15–16 (NIV) says: *"I know your deeds, that you are neither cold nor hot. I wish you were either one or the other! So, because you are lukewarm – neither hot nor cold – I am about to spit you out of my mouth."* Amazing things occur when you have passion. It is a power source from within, which each of us are specifically commanded to bring forth with vigor to propel and empower us to do great things. Passion is the spiritual fervor that ignites your actions and draws others to join in making your vision a reality. In Romans 12:11 (NIV) we find these words: *"Never be lacking in zeal, but keep your spiritual fervor, serving the Lord."* The King James Version puts it this way: *"Not slothful in business; fervent in spirit; serving the Lord."* Clearly, God wants us to be passionate about serving Him and fulfilling the plans we follow for success and prosperity.

ENERGY TO BURN

Passion is the energy that also gives you the confidence to know you can achieve the things you set out to do. Passion is closely related to *desire*. Just as you must desire and want to have the Word of God in your heart to receive His blessings, you must desire to achieve and be a success in your business. Passion is the fire. Passion and desire are what motivate you to act, lead, and persevere. Passion and desire along with a clear vision of what you want to accomplish in business will provide you an unending source of energy to reach your goals.

Will you have down days? Of course you will. But the point is to never let the fire of passion go out of your desire to reach your goals and achieve success. If you feel your passion needs a little rekindling, memorize and meditate on Philippians 4:13 (NKJV) that says: *"I can do all things through Christ who strengthens me."* Because you will grow in confidence for in the things you are doing through Christ, I am confident you will become consistently more passionate in the process. There is no better example of passion for Christ being exhibited than what is reflected in the Apostle Paul. Consider what he wrote in Philippians 3:7-9 (NIV):

> But whatever were gains to me I now consider loss for the sake of Christ. What is more, I consider everything a loss because of the surpassing worth of knowing my Lord, for whose sake I have lost all things. I consider them garbage, that I may gain Christ and be found in him, not having a righteousness of my own that comes from the law, but that which is through faith in Christ—the righteousness that comes from God on the basis of faith.

In this age of social media lingo such as "BFF" (best friends forever), "TTYL" (talk to you later), and "LOL" (laughing out loud), I've joined the bandwagon, too. I describe passion as "IEG" (Internal Excitement Generator). As an "IEG," passion motivates you to perform whatever tasks are before you, no matter how menial, as long as the tasks move you toward your goals and vision. I'm often asked, "How can I nurture my passion?" You nurture passion by first identifying fruitful desires of your heart, and second, by setting goals to make those desires a reality. Desires of the heart may come from an idea or something meaningful you enjoy doing; that you're good at or have developed an expertise in. They may also come from a revelation about something, or even an epiphany. You embrace each opportunity to perform the tasks, which moves you closer to the goals you've set and the vision you have. With each task you successfully accomplish, celebrate it and watch your passion grow!

Anthony Redmon is an outstanding former offensive lineman who played for Auburn University and in the National Football League for the Atlanta Falcons and Arizona Cardinals, who openly professed Christ throughout his eight-year career. He was also an active member of Athletes in Action. Athletes in Action is a global Christian sports ministry working with college and professional athletes to use the platform of sports to help people strengthen their faith. It is also a ministry of Campus Crusade for Christ. During a recent conversation with me, Anthony described passion this way:

> *"Passion for the game inhabits every fabric of your being. It pumps you up and consumes you completely. It demands attention to detail no matter the challenge. It motivates you to push yourself when there's nothing left in the tank. It motivates you to perform through unbearable pain. To perform at the*

highest level, you can never let the fire of passion go out. Passion is the thing that gets you up in the morning. When your body is telling you to stop, passion is what drives you to keep going. Passion pushes you beyond anything your human mind can tell you. Passion tells you to never stop, never quit, and never give up!"

PASSION IS CONTAGIOUS

People with passion welcome the tasks and challenges before them in route to their goals. They view challenges as opportunities. Here's a paradigm-shifting secret about passion. It is actually the tasks themselves that provide the nourishment and fuel that feeds the passion! With every task a person with passion accomplishes, their passion is sustained and energized. Their goals and vision are affirmed and reaffirmed with each small victory. They remain filled with excitement and develop an insatiable appetite to accomplish even more tasks that move them closer to their goals. That's why what seems like work to others comes so naturally and effortlessly to a person who has passion. They have tapped into their own God-given, self-motivating cycle of "NMP" (Nurturing My Passion). Others around them become excited and want to join and share in the vision. They see confidence and what that passionate person is able to accomplish.

Another secret of passionate people is they are actually having fun on the journey. I'm sure you've heard someone describe what they do for a living and then say, "And I actually get paid for doing this!" The next time you hear that, seek the person out immediately. This is a person who has great passion. Talk to him or her, if you can, or Google and read about them. Check out their spiritual foundation, and if you are comfortable enough and have the opportunity, pick their brain and find out what makes them tick. You will gain great insight into what passion is all about and how you can benefit more from nurturing and feeding your passion.

Passion is sometimes difficult to describe, but it works like an elixir that promises all who taste it that they are on their way to reaching their goals and finding success. It gives you a boldness that puts your actions on autopilot. Often you will not be aware of the energy you are exerting or who is observing your actions. Several years ago, I received a Christmas gift from one of my assistants that has become a favorite gift of mine. Before I unwrapped it, Zerbranitta told me it was "a portrait" of me. I confess I was not too excited about having to put a large portrait of myself up in the office to avoid hurting her feelings. But when I opened it, to my relief, no picture! What was "the portrait?" It was hundreds of clippings of words and phrases from newspaper and magazine articles about activities and events I had been involved with. She had painstakingly cut out words and phrases that described me and pasted them in a large portrait-size frame. Some of the words and phrases included were: *motivated, positive, leadership, service, high level, road to success, not afraid, vision, religion, family, a whole new line of thinking, responsibility, friendly, tactical, always try to get it for you*, and *trust*. Needless to say, this was a real Kodak moment (I'm dating myself) for me and allowed me to see myself much deeper than any photograph could ever have revealed. It was my first experience with a vision board, but one that was prepared through someone else's eyes.

I was grateful to Zerbranitta for her thoughtful and creative gift. What gave me further cause for thought was the idea that the passion I exhibited had motivated her to take the time to meticulously prepare such a unique gift. She went well beyond what I ever expected to receive as a gift. Passion is like that. As most professional athletes and peak performers will tell you, passion pushes you to go beyond the limits of ordinary human expectations.

AVOID PASSION-KILLERS

Beware, of "passion-killers" – naysayers, doubters, and haters who try to convince you that your hopes, dreams, and goals are unrealistic. They want to shape your concept of what *you* should think about *your* abilities. Even when they are not speaking, they can drain your energy because you sense their disbelief. I recently listened to a sermon by Bishop T.D. Jakes where the title said it all: "You Don't Have to Believe in My Dream." That's exactly how you have to respond to passion-killers. Some of them even get satisfaction out of dousing the fire of your passion. You should have no hesitation about leaving passion-killers behind. Matthew 10:14 (NKJV) tells us: *"And whoever will not receive you nor hear your words, when you depart from that house or city, shake off the dust from your feet."*

I heard a friend tell a story about a known passion-killer who was in a group she was speaking to, but she did not want to identify him by name. Cleverly seizing the moment she said, "You know there are just some people who light up a room when they come in. And then," she paused, "there are others where the room lights up when they leave... Which are you?" Avoid passion-killers and avoid sharing your goals and vision with them. If the passion-killer is someone close to you, take it to God in prayer – praying together along with the other person, if possible. Ask the other person to continually pray for you, and you continually pray for them. Meditate on scriptures such as Psalm 37:5 that says: *"Commit your way to the LORD, Trust also in Him, and He shall bring it to pass."*

My youngest brother, Kelvin, became the oldest rookie to play in the American Basketball Association when he debuted at age forty-seven during the 2007 season.[50] Kelvin was featured on CNN's *Headline News* and other major news outlets. As a result of his tenacity for the game of basketball, he was invited to tryout for D-League teams owned by the Denver Nuggets, Dallas Mavericks, and Utah Jazz. I asked Kelvin about the role that passion played for him on his journey. This is what he told me:

> *"Passion gives you a youthful heart and an energetic spirit. When you have passion, much like the younger generation, you ignore things... Things like age, odd stares, and comments that ordinarily prevent you from having the boldness to take the actions necessary to reach your goals. My dream,*

since junior high school, was to play in the National Basketball Association. In the years following my college career, the passion in my heart compelled me to keep my dream alive. I never gave up on that dream. I stayed in shape, ate right, and played lots of pick-up games. My message wherever I go is to tell the young and old: Don't let anyone convince you to smother your passion and never give up on your dreams. You never know what God has in store for you."

Today, Kelvin is passionately preaching the Gospel of Jesus Christ and was blessed to take God's message to Africa recently. Whatever else you do, by all means, have passion!

POWER POINTS

- You must have passion for your business and personal life goals.
- To be passionate in business, you must be doing something you enjoy – something that you are good at or have an expertise in.
- Passion comes from the heart and moves you to action.
- God's Word tells us not to be lukewarm, but have passion and zeal in our endeavors and service to Him.
- Passion is contagious.
- Avoid passion-killers, naysayers, doubters, and haters.
- Tap into your passion. Let it energize you.

PART IV.

DO IT NOW!

Tomorrow is not promised to me. The time God has given me is a day less than what I had yesterday. I refuse to procrastinate or give myself excuses not to identify, prioritize and complete daily, the important tasks necessary to attain the success and abundance God has promised me. I will take action now to use the gifts and resources He provides not just for my benefit, but to be a blessing to others. I understand that to whom much is given, much is required!

Reference:

James 4:14

Psalm 90:12

Jeremiah 29:11

Luke 12:48 (NKJV)

Chapter 6

TAKE ACTION

He who observes the wind will not sow, and he who regards the clouds will not reap. Ecclesiastes 11:4 (NKJV)

SECRET #6: SUCCESSFUL ENTREPRENEURS TAKE ACTION

They don't procrastinate. Everything in this book is about taking action...now! The scripture reference above says it all. If all you do is daydream and watch the clouds, then all you can ever expect to be is a daydreamer. If you are one who, after careful study and planning, refuses to take action, you can expect to never reap the benefits that come with being a successful entrepreneur. You will never move beyond your present circumstance. Waiting for the perfect time to take action means you will always be waiting. Whatever the direction you feel called to go in, the time is now for you to say to yourself: "No more excuses!" James 4:14 says: "*Why, you do not even know what will happen tomorrow. What is your life? You are a mist that appears for a little while and then vanishes".* It is time for you to have courage, exercise self-discipline over your life, prepare to make a difference in the lives of others and step outside your comfort zone today!

Successful people don't whittle their time away daydreaming or wondering what might have been. Have you ever come up with a neat gadget you thought would be useful and could make you a lot of money? Chances are sometime later you saw that gadget in a store or on TV and said to yourself, "There goes my idea. I could have been selling those things." The only difference between you and the person who brought the gadget to market is that person took action. Consider for a moment:

- What if Bill Gates had never started Microsoft?
- What if Ray Crock had never started McDonalds?
- What if Steve Jobs had not pursued his dream after dropping out of college?

These were people of action.

It's OK to dream. It's OK and necessary to have faith, but in conjunction with your dreams and faith, you must also act. The Bible says, *"Faith without works is dead."*[51] Talk with all the people you need to talk to. Gather as much information as you can about what it will take to support the business you are in or contemplating. Become an expert in your chosen field. But after gathering the information you need, plan accordingly, take action, and have faith in knowing your action will lead to the results you desire!

IT'S REALLY FEAR

Procrastination is the first cousin of fear and a great killer of dreams. Putting things off provides an excuse not to take action. Procrastination robs you of energy and valuable time. *Time* has been described as a "nonrenewable resource."[52] Once it's gone, it's gone. You can never get time back. Proverbs 27:1 says: *"Do not boast about tomorrow, for you do not know what a day may bring."* Don't allow procrastination to lull you into a do-nothing, excuse-filled attitude. If you look deeper you'll find what procrastination really is. It's a nice way of saying you are scared. You are fearful. You have fear of the unknown. You have a fear of failure. You may even have fear of success and what that would bring. Procrastination, and thus fear feeds on itself. The more you procrastinate, the more fearful and likely you will continue to procrastinate and be fearful. Break the cycle by honestly facing your fears and taking them to God in prayer first. Then set goals and take action each day to reach those goals. You must take some action every day toward making your business a reality or a well-oiled profit generating machine. You must literally tell yourself what action you are going to take, then commit to get it done. Right now, think back one (1) year ago today. Imagine what you could have accomplished by now had you taken action on things you contemplated just 12 short months ago. Waiting for the perfect time to start your business means you will never start. Waiting for the perfect time to make critical decisions that will grow your business means you will never grow. Waiting for the perfect time to do strategic planning means you will never plan. Waiting for the perfect time to develop innovative new products and services means you will be left behind. Success requires *"DPA"* – deliberate, persistent action. Stop right now and write down on the lines below (or on your mobile device or computer) where you would like to be 12 months from today in your personal life; in your finances and in your business.

_____

_____

_____

If you wrote out your goals, you have taken the first step to overcoming procrastination and becoming a person of action. If you did not, bookmark this spot and write those things out in the next 24 hours.

Whenever I have a task that I can find all kinds of excuses to put off, I motivate myself to action by repeating one word to myself. That word is *journey, journey, journey.* It comes from that Chinese proverb I mentioned earlier that says "the 'journey' of a thousand miles begins with one step." By taking that first step, I am that much closer to my destination. With each step, the *journey* gets easier and easier.

For example, after many years of being out of school, I pondered a decision to go back to school and get my MBA. I dreaded the many hours of study, exams, and reports that I would inevitably have to do. I procrastinated and used the excuse that I was too busy with my consulting business and legal work. But I found a great executive MBA program at Auburn University Montgomery and once I took that initial step and got into the coursework, the time seemed to fly. Less than two years after I graduated, I was blessed to be named one of Auburn University Montgomery's Top 40 Graduates along with such inductees as General Richard Meyers, who served as the chairman of the Joint Chiefs of Staff. He was appointed by President George W. Bush to lead the Joint Chiefs right after the events of "9/11" occurred. My decision to take action not only resulted in my earning a MBA, it enabled me to have the wonderful experience of crossing paths with General Meyers and other distinguished graduates of the program.

OPPORTUNITIES FOR LEARNING

In taking action, there will be times when things don't turn out exactly as planned. But that is no reason to quit or abort your pursuit of success in business. Running into obstacles is actually a part of your growth and maturation as a business owner. In reality, obstacles are opportunities for learning.

Whether the plans you take action on go off without a hitch, or they get temporarily derailed, take a page from how the military does it. Following every significant engagement, event, or activity, they have what is called a "debriefing." It is a formally structured process where they study the outcomes of the situation. With unabashed candor, they examine the good, the bad, and the ugly of what happened. They document the positive and negative "take-a-ways." They build on what they learn and discard what does not work. They operate in a state of *continuous improvement*. Regardless of what anyone says, our military is the best on the planet, and we can thank God for that. In order to be in a state of *continuous improvement* in your personal life or in business, you must constantly take action.

A quote on a graduation card given to me by my Great Aunt Lela Perry, when I obtained my undergraduate degree from Alabama State University was a constant motivator for me to remain in a state of *continuous improvement* from that day on. I thought about this phrase during those late nights of study for my law degree and MBA. Each time I asked myself, why am I doing this, the quote by Henry Wadsworth Longfellow would come to mind. It reads: "*The heights of great men reached and kept were not attained by sudden flight, but they, while their companions slept, were toiling upward in the night.*" Success requires you to take action regardless of what others around you may be doing or not doing.

As a side note, my mother, a retired school teacher, is a woman not afraid to take action and was also about continuously improving herself. In 1975, we marched together as she was awarded a master's degree and I received my undergraduate degree from Alabama State University.

One of the biggest reasons I believe most people fail to take action and reach the levels of success available to them is "rationalization." In other words, they rationalize or convince themselves they have a good excuse or reason for failing to take the action necessary to move from their present circumstance. The reality is they lack the discipline and self-control to do what is necessary now (by planting the right seeds today) in order to reap the benefits of success and prosperity (the harvest) later. Galatians 5:22–23 speaks of the Christ-like characteristics of "forbearance" and "self-control" that we should all ascribe to. Rather than face the fact that we don't have the discipline and self-control to take action necessary for our success, we evade the real issue and take the easy way out – we rationalize. Once again, a spin on Albert Einstein's definition of insanity is appropriate here. That is, *doing the same thing over and over again and <u>lacking the self-discipline to "take action" that is necessary to bring about</u> a different result.* Proverbs 25:28 tells us when you lack self-control, not only are your own actions undisciplined, you are susceptible, and even attract, negative outside influences that control your life. So don't be a weak-minded undisciplined person. The Message version puts verse 28 this way: *"A person without self-control is like a house with its doors and windows knocked out."* In other words, you lack control over what comes into your life and what goes out.

The question for you is, "What rationalizations and excuses have you used to hold yourself back from taking action toward a better life for yourself? Is it because you are a woman? Is it because of your ethnicity, where you live, or where you grew up? Is it because you have no money or lost your job? Have you convinced yourself that no one will be interested in what you have to say? Is it because you feel you will miss out on something if you commit and take action now? Do you try to blame others like your boss, supervisor, friends, or even your parents for your inaction? I'm sure you can list other "excuses" and "rationalizations," but don't allow yourself to fall into that trap. Be conscious of this tendency within yourself, and aware that your failure to act may be due to shortcomings in other areas of your life such as the fear of failure or the acceptance of mediocrity. Second Peter 1:5–6 says: *"For this very reason, make every effort to add to your faith, goodness; and to goodness, knowledge; and to knowledge, self-control; and to self-control, perseverance; and to perseverance, godliness."* Success and a prosperous life are yours for the taking, but you must be intentional and committed to your success. That means you must exercise the self-control and discipline to take the actions necessary to have that life. Daydreaming about it or having a victim's attitude won't get you there.

Let's look at the story of Raymond Bruce. Perhaps there has been a traumatic event in your life that you feel is a good excuse or rationalization for doing nothing with your life. This certainly could have been the case for Raymond, a former martial arts student I taught. Raymond was one of my most gifted students. He had one of the fastest roundhouse back kicks you ever wanted to see. Prior to finishing college, Raymond decided to join the United States Army and serve his country. During a training mission, a track on the eleven-man Anti-Personnel Carrier he was riding broke and the vehicle wrecked. Raymond was severely injured. His spine was crushed and the spinal cord partially severed at the C-6 and C-7 vertebra. He lost use of both legs and motion in his hands. Raymond could have lived on a disability check only for the rest of his life, but his desire to *receive* and *achieve* all that God had in store for him was un-phased. He exercised discipline and self-control, which enabled him to move beyond the circumstances of this terrible accident. He persevered through a year and a half of gruelling rehab.

Following rehab, Raymond was able to gain a level of functional independence and he re-entered college. He obtained his undergraduate degree from Alabama State in 1982, a master's degree from Auburn University Montgomery in 1985 and a doctorate degree from Word of Life Bible School of Marshall, Texas, in 2009. In 1985, Raymond began working for Easter Seals where he was a catalyst in working with former Montgomery Mayor Emory Folmar and former City Councilman Joe Reed to upgrade Montgomery's city codes to make public buildings and sidewalks wheel chair accessible. His own personal escapades included visiting public establishments such as restaurants and office buildings where he could not gain access in a wheel chair. Raymond politely put the owners "on notice" that the lack of access into their buildings excluded an entire population and could expose them to legal liability and fines. He got results.

In 1992, Raymond began work for the Paralyzed Veterans of America (PVA), a non-profit organization whose mission is to assist and empower paralyzed veterans in achieving independence and freedom. As a senior national service officer and senior benefits advocate for PVA, Raymond traveled joyfully around the country advocating for paralyzed veterans and providing guidance regarding benefits and available programs. Until his recent retirement, Raymond did not let his circumstance become an excuse not to act.

He had an attitude that did not view his circumstance as an obstacle. He took action, and as a result, thousands of America's finest service men and women are benefitting from his example, efforts and actions with PVA. [Also see, *Attitude Determines Altitude*, p. 119]

ON THE SHOULDERS OF OTHERS

When it comes to teaching others to take action in business, I must acknowledge several people whose coaching, marketing, and training I've studied for some time. They are John Maxwell, Brendon Burchard, Eben Pagan, Brian Tracy, John Eggen, George C. Fraser, and Karl Bryan, pioneers and leaders in online marketing, entrepreneurship, coaching, mentoring, and networking. These individuals are, as self-made billionaire Michael V. Roberts would call them, "Actionaires." They are visionary people who are doers and born to change the world.[53]

It would have been nice to have had their training when I started one of the first world's first consumer online information businesses in 1986, The IMFAX Corporation®. The problem was that fewer than ten (10%) percent of Americans knew what a personal computer (PC) was or had ever heard of the Internet. IBM had introduced the first PC only five years earlier, in August 1981.[54] Surveys I took revealed people simply did not believe I could provide information to them, on virtually any topic, in just hours from a computer. God gave me a vision of things to come. I took action and started an online information business that is just now bearing fruit. Success does not happen by accident. You must have a vision of where you want to go, plan and set goals, have the courage to step out, and finally, take action. You never know where your action will lead. Michael Dell started Dell Computers just two years before I started The IMFAX Corporation®. Had I met Michael back then, rather than fifteen years later during a visit he made to Montgomery in 2001, you could be typing on a "Davis-Dell" computer today (hmm... has a nice ring to it). Success follows entrepreneurs who are not afraid to take action!

SPOTTING THE WAVES OF CHANGE

Spotting the waves of change so you are able to profit from that change requires taking action on the right things. You must not only take action by climbing the ladder to the top. You must be certain your ladder is leaning against the right wall. Influential Author Stephen R. Covey puts it this way, "If the ladder is <u>not</u> leaning against the right wall, every step we take just gets us to the wrong place faster." Building on what Dr. Covey says, I would add: *if your ladder **is** against the **right** wall, every step you take gets you to the **right** place faster.... <u>and ahead of the pack</u>*.

Great success awaits those who are able to spot the waves of change, take action and get ahead of the waves to welcome the crowd with their innovations. Andrew Carnegie recognized, before most in the industry, the importance of chemistry in steel making and the benefits of the "Bessemer, Thomas basic, and open-hearth processes" to make steel. He saw how the process would bring about major change in the way and speed in which steel was made. Being one of the first to take advantage of the new processes became key to his success as a steel manufacturer and made him one of the wealthiest men in the world.[55] Steve Jobs hinted at the concept of the iPhone in 2003, well before it was released in 2007. His iconic status as a visionary and innovator is well documented. Jobs could not only spot the waves of change, he often influenced the speed at which the wave traveled as demonstrated by his unparalleled innovative *system for product launches*. Releasing of Apple's products was more than just generating hype. Those who have waited in long lines for hours just to buy an iPhone or iPad know what I'm talking about. Steve Jobs relied heavily on the insights of Alabama native Tim Cook, in spotting trends, creating waves of change and recognizing the next big things. Tim, is the new CEO of Apple and earned a degree in industrial engineering from Auburn in 1983.

Being able to spot trends and waves of change is a different level of knowledge combined with sharp instincts and good judgment. This is particularly true today with the exponential rate at which change is occurring and the colossal volumes of new data and information being generated. You have to (a) be able to get above the forest; (b) be able to sift through relevant data; and (c) be able to chart a course where a need will be filled and there is great demand for the innovation. Stephen Covey has said, "A leader is the one who climbs the tallest tree, surveys the entire situation, and then yells, 'Wrong Jungle!'"[56] That's why thousands of people who come up with great ideas fall short so often. They don't evaluate their ideas objectively based on the formula above, then flavor it with their own instincts or business acumen.

Nowhere is change occurring faster than in business and technology. Knowing when to take action to start or grow your business are in and of themselves great challenges. Less than five years ago, most people had never heard of social media giants such as Facebook, LinkedIn, YouTube and Twitter. Heck, most people didn't know what "social media" was. What's worse is, before people can get their arms around the existing social media tools, along comes another batch such as Google+, Pinterest, Tumblr and Instagram which are gaining in popularity. We also have choices of which Internet search engine to use, such as Google, Yahoo, or Bing, through which we gather needed information. Being able to spot trends and change is important to business survival and longevity.

Speaking of "being able to get above the forest", small-business owners will be happy to know tools are now available to help manage your social media and promote your business without wasting hours of time online. Two popular do-it-yourself tools that have been around awhile are Hootsuite (http://hootsuite.com) and Sendible (http://sendiblee.com). These sites let you post, promote and monitor all your social media sites on a dashboard and engage your audience, prospects and customers in as little or as much time as you want to spend. You can even automate communications. If you want the option of more hands-on support, there is a site called Social Media Delivered at http://socialmediadelivered.com. Of course, there are many others on the horizon.

CHRIST AND SOCIAL NETWORKING

While we are on the subject of trends and social media, I want to bring the focus around to who I would say, without a doubt, is the originator of change via social media and social networking. I can also identify the search engine that was used. The person is Jesus Christ and His search engine was and remains the Holy Spirit. In saving and transforming humanity, Jesus Christ was and is the greatest social-networking guru of all time. He started with twelve disciples and taught them about salvation and the purpose for their lives through parables and by His example. The ancient mysterious tool he used to teach them was *"word-of-mouth."* On the Internet, information spreads by *"word of mouse."*[57] The disciples delivered Jesus' message of salvation throughout the world. But before they went forth, Christ left them the world's first and most powerful search engine ever, the Holy Spirit. As a result, we have direct access to God.[58] Just as the search engines like Google and Bing go out and search the Internet for information and bring back the results, so it is with the Holy Spirit. It searches the mind of God and reveals its truths to man. Just as one seeks information by entering a query in a search engine, we enter a "query" for God's truths through the Holy Spirit by prayer. Just as you must be plugged into the Internet to receive information from the World Wide Web, you must also be plugged into the Holy Spirit to receive God's guidance and direction. To get plugged into the Internet, you need a computer or mobile device. To get plugged into to the Holy Spirit, you need to pray and to receive Christ in your heart. In 1 Corinthians 2:10–14, we can see just how closely the Holy Spirit works like a powerful Internet search engine to reveal God's truths to us:

> *These are the things God has revealed to us by his Spirit. The Spirit searches all things, even the deep things of God. For who knows a person's thoughts except their own spirit within them? In the same way no one knows the thoughts of God except the Spirit of God. What we have received is not the spirit of the world, but the Spirit who is from God, so that we may understand what God has freely given us. This is what we speak, not in words taught us by human wisdom but in words taught by the Spirit, explaining spiritual realities with Spirit-taught words. The person without the Spirit does not accept the things that come from the Spirit of God but considers them foolishness, and cannot understand them because they are discerned only through the Spirit.*

In a sermon entitled, "*Gaining Insight Into God's Word,*" Pastor David Jeremiah described how the Holy Spirit performs a search and reveals God's truths. The analogy Pastor Jeremiah used was that of a federal customs official. Pastor Jeremiah's sermon predates the existence of Google, but citing Romans 2:27 and Revelation 2:23, what he says is most enlightening:

> *In the New Testament the word "search" is a word which is used like we would describe a custom's official going through someone's bags looking for hidden articles. And the word tells us that the Holy Spirit, who has been given to us who are Christians, explores the deep treasures of God like he was "searching" for lost articles and then he takes those deep treasures of God and he reveals those truths which God had in store for those who love him and the process of spiritual illumination is something that we receive, not something we achieve.*

In 2 Chronicles 16:9, we find the story of Asa, King of Judah being reminded of how the Holy Spirit searches the earth for people committed to Him. After having relied totally on God for his victories at the beginning of his reign, Asa later turned away from God and began to rely on the military power of man. A prophet rebuked the king and reminded him, "*For the eyes of the LORD range throughout the earth to strengthen those whose hearts are fully committed to him. You have done a foolish thing, and from now on you will be at war.*"

The next time someone asks you who started the social media explosion you can tell them it was Jesus Christ. You can also tell them His search engine of choice was the Holy Spirit. But don't take my word for it. Let's go to the source. In Acts 1:8 Christ spoke these words.

> *But you will receive power when the Holy Spirit comes on you; and you will be my witnesses in Jerusalem, and in all Judea and Samaria, and to the ends of the earth.*

It is truly amazing how these words which Christ spoke over 2000 years ago reign true today. He assured us that we would receive power after we receive the Holy Spirit and then become witnesses for Him "in Jerusalem" and "to the ends of the earth." No one knew about social networking back then. Neither could anyone have imagined at that time how the Gospel would be spread to "the ends of the earth" without in-person contact. But Christ knew and now we know that through the advent of technology such as email the Internet, smart phones, etc, we can be witnesses for Him "in Jerusalem" and "to the ends of the earth," in an instant!

I included the verse from Acts 1:8 above because it was the "Verse for the Day" on my YouVersion Bible during the exact time period I was emailing fellow church member Duane Donner, who was on a mission sabbatical "in Jerusalem" as a witness for Christ. I shared the verse with him on July 26, 2013. The words of Jesus Christ in this verse spoke to me plainly and loudly to confirm that He clearly knew of things to come 2000 years ago. Wasn't it Noah who was instructed by God to build a strange boat called an "Ark" in order to prepare for something Noah had never heard of before called "rain"? Noah was obedient. (Hebrews 11:7) We have the benefit now, through the passage of time and through the Holy Spirit, in knowing that God will allow for the creation of the vehicles and modalities through which His purposes will be fulfilled, in His time. Our part is to obey and be a witness for Him in spreading the Good News "to the ends of the earth as the that scripture calls for."

When Acts 1:8 also appeared in our pastor's message on Sunday, July 28, 2013, two days after I shared it with Duane who was in Jerusalem, I said in my mind, *"OK Lord, I'm putting this in the book."* I also included a link to the same eye-opening message Pastor Chris Hodges delivered that day entitled, *"Change Your World–One Person at a Time"*. It was viewed live from the Church of the Highlands website in many states and countries around the world. It can also be viewed right now online at: www.churchofthe-highlands.com/media/message/one-person-at-a-time. This is literally the last story I inserted in this book on July 29, 2013 before sending it off to press. We serve an amazing God!

Back on the subject of spotting trends and the waves of change, here are my top ten pointers:

1. Get above the forest.
2. Develop a leader's bias to test new information against your own knowledge and instincts. [59]
3. Follow global trends in your industry, niche or areas of interest.
4. Read magazines, books, blogs, ezines (digital magazines), etc., about your industry or area of interest.
5. Be sensitive to buying habits, shifts in those habits and overall demand.

6. Determine the conversation going on in your customers' heads and join it.
7. Expand your view of your place in the world.
8. Stick with what you know and understand.
9. Establish objective criteria or targets to measure adverse changes or opportunities for your business.
10. Rely on the Holy Spirit to guide you. He knows what is coming!

POWER POINTS

- Take action now.
- Procrastination feeds on itself. Break the cycle.
- It's OK to dream and have faith, but God requires you to act to be successful.
- Putting things off provides an excuse not to act. "Tomorrow" is not your friend.
- Time is a non-renewable resource. Once it's gone, it's gone. Don't waste it.
- A failed action that you do take is an opportunity for learning how *not* to do something.
- Build on failed actions. They are building blocks for success.
- Don't "rationalize." It is the process of convincing yourself you have a good excuse not to take action to reach your goals.
- Be certain your ladder is leaning against the right wall.
- Get above the forest.
- Interacting with social media is now a way of life for any business. Find the right "affordable" social media management tool and get on board.
- Be aware of trends that can affect your business, positively or negatively.
- Rely on the Holy Spirit to guide you.

PART V.

YOUR SECRET SAUCE: THE FRUIT OF THE SPIRIT

The key to my success is relationships. First is my relationship with God. I will love God with all my heart, soul and mind. I will strive to be more Christ-like as I embrace the characteristics of love, joy and peace. Second is my relationship with others. I will love my neighbor as myself. I will exercise forbearance [restraint], kindness and goodness in building relationships. I will be faithful to engage only in business dealings that benefit all involved, will exercise gentleness in the use of power and be self-disciplined to do what is necessary to reach and exceed my desired goals with excellence and integrity.

Reference:
Matthew 22:37-39:
Galatians 5:22-25
1 Corinthians 12:30-31

Chapter 7

GOOD JUDGMENT

Good judgment wins favor, but the way of the unfaithful leads to their destruction

Proverbs 13:15 (NIV)

SECRET #7: SUCCESSFUL ENTREPRENEURS USE GOOD JUDGMENT

Every day in your business, you are going to be called upon to make decisions. In order to make good decisions, you must use good judgment. Every decision you make will affect some aspect of your business, either positively or negatively, including the employees you hire, how you handle conflict, the contracts you negotiate, the deals you find, where you choose to market your product or services, and the partners you take on. All these things require that you use good judgment on a consistent basis to be successful. Will you make mistakes? Yes! But having good judgment means you also learn from your mistakes. Pray for God to grant you wisdom in your decision-making process. Read the Book of Proverbs (one chapter a day) and prepare to grow in wisdom and stature in your business dealings.

The key to using good judgment is acquiring knowledge while effectively using the knowledge you have gained. It is impossible to make good decisions if you have not acquired the knowledge necessary to make an informed decision. It's a given. The success of your business depends upon the decisions you make. Truly successful people have a self-awareness of this reality. This means get in the habit of embracing four basic principles:

- Gather relevant facts.
- Consider wise advice and input of others.
- Consider circumstances and consequences of your actions.
- Take clear decisive action.

GARBAGE IN, GARBAGE OUT

You've heard the old saying about getting good results from information you enter into your computer. If the data you input is bad, the results or output you get will likewise be bad. Successful leaders will tell you they did not get to where they are alone. They will also tell you they had the input of other smart people. Obtaining wise counsel from others is a necessary ingredient to ensure the successful execution of your plans.[60] Be the kind of leader who encourages open and honest dialogue, even if it seems critical of your decisions or you don't agree with it. If the people around you are always saying yes to you and agreeing with whatever you say, watch out! They are setting you up for failure. When you hear someone say, "John has really good business instincts," what they are really telling you is that John does his homework, studies, is always prepared, and makes wise decisions that are known to benefit his business. [61]

Using good judgment is also equated with having wisdom. Wisdom is a gift from God. You must pray to receive wisdom and endeavor to make wise decisions in all you do.[62] There is great success that follows wisdom. As stated in Chapter 2, when God gave King Solomon an opportunity to ask for whatever he wanted, Solomon asked for wisdom to lead the people. God answered his prayer by not only granting him wisdom, but great wealth and prosperity as well.[63] By exercising wisdom and good judgment in the decisions you make, you will gain respect from your employees, suppliers, competition, and all those with whom you come into contact.

Using good judgment comes into play even when making decisions in the early stages of a new business. I was recently mentoring a young entrepreneur who had started a business and was filled with excitement over the prospects of getting large contracts in the near future. He had a good paying job, but wanted to quit the job to spend more time working in his new business, even though it had not begun to generate revenue. He felt the business was not serving any purpose because it was not making money.

I asked him two questions, based on the type business he was in.

Question #1: Do you have enough savings to sustain you and your family for six months?

"No," he replied.

Question #2: Are you aware that because you have a business, there are expenses and deductions that benefit you directly and can reduce your personal income tax liability, even though your business is not generating much revenue at this point? These are things you want to discuss with an accountant, but again he replied, "No."

The first question brought home the obvious realization of problems he would create by quitting his job too soon. There are situations where six months may not be the magic number, but for him and his success, it was important that he use *good judgment* in deciding when to quit his job and spend full time in the new business.

The second question is one many small-business owners miss altogether. For my mentee, it was an eye-opening revelation to beginning to understand the basic tenets of operating a business beyond the simple (but supremely important) notion of "making money." Though he was not making a profit, the business expenses he generated as a limited liability company provided deductions for him that would ultimately lower his tax liability. For the first time, in the early stages of his business, he could now begin to think *"strategically"* and begin to develop a "30,000-foot-view" of his approach to growing his business. He could not contain his excitement and said, in the short span of our conversation, his mind was being flooded with new thoughts of how he could more confidently set a course for a transition into the new business. He expressed that much of his anxiety had been about not knowing what "next steps" to plan for and take.

BE A STRATEGIC THINKER

Being a strategic thinker is a vital part of using good judgment. As a small- business owner, my mentee's new thought process was how he could lay the important groundwork for understanding the critical difference between "working in the business" and "working on the business." Initially in every small business, the owners wear many hats and frequently, all the hats. They have no alternative but to "work in the business," performing the day-to-day internal activities of the operation. Working "on the business" is the owner's focus on external factors such as marketing, business development and customer relations to make certain the business has customers and clients continually buying their products and services. It's about hiring the right people and implementing the best systems and processes to grow the business to generate greater revenue and higher profits. The right systems can make a business very scalable, which is when rapid growth can occur in a relatively short period of time. If you remain stuck in the weeds of day-to-day operations of tasks that could easily be delegated, this can be a reflection of your judgment and desire to really move your business forward.

The truth is many small-business owners have difficulty letting go of some of the hats they wear which leaves little or no time to "work on the business" and secure new customers. They continue to micro-manage all aspects of the operation because they believe no one can do it better than they can. They may be correct in some sense, but they are not using good judgment. Their actions often stifle the efforts of good employees, and in a single blow, can also consume valuable time that could be used for mining new customers and business opportunities. It goes without saying that one must hire competent and motivated employees. However, the ability to *truly* delegate is a major inhibitor to many businesses on the path to success.

Having good judgment and using it can be a valuable tool to customer relations and growing your business. An interesting statistic to be aware of is for many businesses, 70 percent to 80 percent of revenue comes from existing customers and repeat business; a statistic of which Clark Kent, who wrote the Foreword in this book, was very much aware. Clark was performing services for a customer with operations in Dallas and Atlanta. After the contract had been signed, the customer learned of a significant change in requirements that warranted an increase in the revenue to be paid under contract. It was going to be a bureaucratic headache for the customer to get additional funding, and time was of-the-essence. Clark told the customer that it would not be necessary for him to get additional funding, that he would fulfill the additional requirements under the financial terms previously agreed upon. Clark knew that the additional responsibility could be very costly for his company. But rather than conveniently trying to gain a few extra dollars, Clark used this situation as an opportunity to enhance his relationship with the customer. The contract was performed flawlessly to the customer's delight, and Clark continues to see the fruit of additional business and glowing references from his focus on the relationship rather than on the profit in that instance. The good judgment Clark exercised in this case has paid far more dividends than the extra revenue he could have generated by having the customer jump through the hoops he faced to complete the project.

COUNT THE COST AND DECIDE

I should emphasize that Clark did not just venture out on a lucky guess or take a random chance before agreeing to the additional responsibilities. Using good judgment is much more than that. First, he followed the teachings found in Luke 14:28, which says: *"For which of you, intending to build a tower, does not sit down first and count the cost, whether he has enough to finish it."*

Clark adhered to the four basic principles found in the passage above:

- Gather relevant facts.
- Consider the wise counsel of others.
- Consider the circumstances and consequences of your action.
- Take clear and decisive action.

Good judgment and integrity are two Bible-inspired inner qualities that go hand-in-hand. The more they are exhibited, the easier it becomes to lead and gain influence and power to accomplish your goals.

Here is a final note for budding young entrepreneurs gaining experience working on jobs for other companies. In this age of the Internet and social media, the issue of good judgment often arises as it relates to what you put on social media sites about yourself. Only a few states offer any protection from an employer or school that demands passwords to your social media sites.[64] I encourage any reader who frequents social-media outlets such as Facebook, Twitter, YouTube, Pinterest, Instagram or Tumblr, to exercise good judgment and wisdom regarding anything you post. Negative or unflattering conduct about yourself or others can have a lasting impact on your ultimate success in the business world and the job market in general. Even though you may feel like "everybody is doing it," use discretion and guard your privacy. Be self-aware, which allows you to think independently about what you are exposing about yourself. While there is a "group-think" social-media culture that is calling you to hold nothing back, have the inner fortitude to use good judgment and set yourself apart by being cautious and wise about what you put out there or respond to. You may have deleted it from your computer or mobile device, but remember, it stays out there, "in the cloud."

POWER POINTS

- Use good judgment in making all decisions regarding your business.
- Seek the wisdom of God in your decision-making process.
- Read the book of Proverbs.
- Use good judgment when you hire, handle conflict, and negotiate.
- The judgment you exercise sends a message about who you are.
- Gather all of the facts and consider wise advice and the consequences for action or inaction.
- Be a strategic thinker.
- Develop a retention plan for repeat customers
- Form a community and educate them
- Have a dominating message for your market
- Count the cost and be decisive.

Chapter 8

INTEGRITY

Here is a saying you can trust. If anyone wants to be a leader in the church, he wants to do a good work for God and people. A leader must be free from blame. He must be faithful to his wife. In anything he does, he must not go too far. He must control himself. He must be worthy of respect. He must welcome people into his home. He must be able to teach.

1 Timothy 3:1–2(NIV)

SECRET #8: SUCCESSFUL ENTREPRENEURS HAVE INTEGRITY

Integrity is the secret sauce of networking and building business relationships that translate into higher sales. Have you ever been burned by someone with a business you felt had no integrity? Would you do business with him again? Probably not.

Now think about someone you know who is a person of integrity, someone who stands behind their products and services, and is not out to gouge you. Given the choice between these two, who would you seek to do business with again, or pattern your own business after? Let me guess. Proverbs 11:20 (MSG) says: *"God can't stand deceivers, but oh how he relishes integrity."*

Your reputation and your word are two of the most powerful tools you have in business. You have control over both. The business culture often suggests the way to get ahead is to be callous, ruthless or underhanded. They go for the quick buck at any cost, because it leads to easy money and claim "it's just business." There is a price to pay. Proverbs 14:12 says: *"There is a way that seems right to a man, but in the end it leads to death."* In most cases, gains of those who subscribe to this philosophy are short-lived.[65] Truly successful people know that when you exercise integrity and exhibit Christ-like leadership qualities, you will reap positive returns in business relationships, repeat business, and employee loyalty and longevity.

A major reason people become frustrated as entrepreneurs is that they enter the game already misguided about the paradigms of true success. They fail to understand that success is not about how much you can syphon from customers and clients. It's about relationships and the value you create for them. Questions your customers want to know are: Will it make my life easier? Will it solve my problem or meet my need? It's about added value and customer service. In most situations, the old adage is still true: The customer *is* always right. Certainly, you are in business to make a profit, and you must run your business on sound business principles, but the focus should always be on the customer. Yet never let profits over people be the driving force behind how you operate in business. Remember this secret from John Maxwell, *"People don't care how much you know, until they know how much you care."* The integrity and concern you exhibit toward the customer could very well be the competitive advantage that will help you keep that customer for a long time. It goes back to a Christ-centered definition of an entrepreneur cited in the Introduction:

> "An entrepreneur is one who serves others in the marketplace through the offering of his or her goods and wares that create value for customers and clients. In other words, an entrepreneur is a solution provider and one who fills the needs of others for compensation. Your primary focus should not be on the selling, even though you do have to sell and be good at it to make money. However, it's not about you or the great products and services you may want to push on customers. It's about serving your customers with integrity and creating sustained value for them that gives you longevity and keeps you creatively focusing on their needs that leads to long-term profitability."

Your ability to become and remain a person of integrity in your business dealings and relationships requires that you constantly desire and maintain a closer relationship with God. It's all you need.

> *As the deer pants for streams of water, so my soul pants for you, my God. My soul thirsts for God, for the living God. When can I go and meet with God?* (Psalm 42:1–2, NIV).

FIRST THINGS FIRST

Having integrity is simply good for the bottom line. Before anyone will want to do business with you on a long-term basis, that customer must know and feel that you are a person of integrity. This is important when networking and building relationships with new customers. Potential customers will not immediately know or care whether or not you are a person of integrity when they initially meet you. So don't blow it starting out. Maya Angelou put it best when she said, *"People will forget what you said. People will forget what you did. But people will never forget how you made them feel."*

Simply because you use the name of God also does not mean you are necessarily a person of integrity, but you never know what impact it will have when you acknowledge that you are a person of faith. Several years ago at a business lunch in Atlanta, I was hosting a group whose business we wanted. Before the meal, I announced, "As soon as your team leader gets back, I'd like to offer a blessing for the food." Thinking he was being helpful, a new senior member of my own team leaned over and whispered: "They don't usually say prayers at this kind of meeting." I gently whispered back, "Since I'm paying, they'll have to get over it." Following lunch, the other company's team leader came over to me and said, "Thank you for offering that prayer. I normally say my blessing under my breath because no one ever openly does it." Needless to say, we formed a business alliance, and I'd like to think one of the reasons was that we were people of integrity.

Marvin Carroll, the president of Tec Masters, often says that if you want to find out if someone is a person of integrity, take him or her out for a round of golf. He says a person absolutely cannot hide who they are on the golf course. A golfer who puts down a score of six when everyone knows it should be an eight, is a person who has some personality traits you may want to avoid. Marvin also says that when you have integrity, you will find "God's DNA" in many blessings that will come your way.

Harold Finch, a retired senior manager for UPS says integrity has always been a core principle which the company proudly extolled among employees. Indeed, he says it's one of the reasons that UPS has enjoyed such great success. Harold says, "The true measure of the integrity of a person is measured by what a person will do, in a given situation, when no one is looking."

Integrity should also be exhibited in how you go about your networking activities. Integrity can have a definite impact on the strength or weakness of relationships you develop. Like everything else I've discussed in this book, you need to be strategic about networking. Just as every small business needs a marketing plan, you also need a networking plan. You need to spend time at events or functions where the opportunity is greatest to meet potential customers or promote your products and services. That requires doing some homework and planning. There is always a plethora of ongoing networking events, conferences, seminars, social activities, business functions, or other occasions for networking to take place. Not all opportunities are created equal, and some can be costly to attend. Select events wisely and know who is attending. You don't want to waste your time and resources at events that will bear little fruit in terms of new potential customers or contacts that can benefit you and your business down the road.

SURE-FIRE NETWORKING TIPS

a) Be yourself. Don't be overly eager to make a hard pitch at the outset. Take some time to connect and search for things in common that you can discuss. You want to come across as being genuine and being a person of integrity. Finding things in common will not only enhance the conversation, but it will give you points to address in follow-up communications.

b) Establish a relationship first. This is a most important objective. It is widely known that people do business with people they know and like. The opportunity to do business with a prospective customer can never get off the ground unless a relationship is established. Polish your people skills, give them your best smile, and be friendly in your discussions.

c) Bring something of value to the table. The most desired outcome of a networking gathering is to have the prospect follow-up and call *you* to discuss and close a deal for your product or service. One of the best ways to increase the chances of a prospect calling you is to be a valuable resource for information they need. Another is to be willing to refer them to potential customers or contacts (direct competitors excluded, however). They will appreciate it and you will strengthen your relationship. Something I like doing at networking events is connecting people I meet to other people at the same event who appear to be a fit for each other. You can try this. It costs you absolutely nothing and generates lots of energy with each introduction. It's a great way to be viewed as someone who knows how to make things happen, that you are friendly and willing to be helpful. That's a lot of valuable capital to receive in the short span of a few minutes at a networking event.

d) Present your thirty-second elevator speech in twenty-five seconds. Some people enjoy hearing themselves talk. That's fine as long as you keep it brief. The real objective is to get that potential customer or contact to do the talking so you can find a way to establish rapport with him or her. Also, a real key to talking with someone is being aware that you have their full attention. Their eyes and body language will tell you a lot.

e) Develop a spirit of listening. How you listen says a lot about you. Are you showing a genuine interest in what the person is saying or are you just waiting for them to finish so you can dominate the conversation? Being a good listener shows respect and empathy for what a person is saying. It can be the difference between whether you truly connect with the person or not.

f) Be energetic and professional in your presentation. Being energetic and professional will send a message about how you feel about yourself and what you are selling. You want to display an inviting personality and confidence, but remember to be yourself.

g) Have professional looking business cards ready to present. There is no excuse today for not having professional looking business cards. Online printers, office supply stores, and copy centers all do business cards inexpensively. The quality of home printers makes it possible to have great cards. For do-it-yourself at home printing, be sure to use smooth-edged non-perforated stock cards. You do yourself a disservice when you hand someone a business card and simultaneously apologize for the card's appearance.

POCKET YOUR ELEVATOR SPEECH

I know it's networking blasphemy, but there are occasions where you should pocket your thirty-second elevator speech. Well, not completely, but you condense it to a one-liner as you speak following your introduction. To explain: When it comes to building your business, nothing beats having a mentor or business coach. Not only can they help you navigate waters they have been through, they can also be a potent networking source of potential customers and high-level contacts. If you can convince a mentor to allow you to tag-along to a business gathering, a one-liner response is all you'll need unless you have the opportunity to engage in further conversation. You do want that one-liner to be inviting enough to keep that person's attention.

I decided to take a mentee to a business gathering that was attended primarily by CEO's and senior executives of local, regional, and global companies. His business was doing quite well and I knew he was prepared to take it to the *next level*. When I introduced him to a prospect, he immediately went into his thirty-second elevator pitch and concluded very politely with, "and I'd love to do some business with you." After the first introduction, I pulled him aside, held up one finger and said to him, "Only give them your one-liner response." That is, tell them the name of your company the kind of business you are in and what you do for your customers. However, be sure to give enough of a description of what you do, but do it all in one brief sentence.

The rest of the evening, including dinner, went off without a hitch. My mentee met several potential customers and teaming partners with whom he could do business. I later explained to him that this was not the type of meeting for sales pitches. This was what I call a "BP-LLC" event – a time to *"Be Professional, Listen, Learn and Connect."* The focus should be on listening and learning. I explained that during the light conversation with each person he met, he should listen and learn as much as possible while being engaging, of course. Once he had the introduction, a business card in hand or contact info, he had all he needed to start building relationships. A smart thing to do before an introduction is to do a little research on the prospective customer or teaming partner. Your research might reveal that you may be able to connect the prospect with other business opportunities in addition to yourself. Remember, it's about creating value in the relationship. With research in hand you are ready for a follow-up call for a one-on-one meeting or lunch.

Three major takeaways here are:

1. Know that high-level meetings like this take place all the time.
2. If you are fortunate enough to get invited to one, act like you are supposed to be there.
3. Stay close to the person who invited you.

FIND A MENTOR

Having a mentor is an invaluable secret to success. Mentors not only open doors, but they can help you avoid some of the pitfalls and mistakes they made in growing their businesses. Write out your list of potential mentors or people you already know who could be game-changers for your business. Approach them about mentoring. If mentoring is out, ask for an occasional meeting or lunch to get their insights. Many business people who have been around awhile are often willing to impart some level of wisdom and guidance if you can get on their schedules. The idea is to get a significant introduction or referral of a potential customer. But if your relationship is such that they allow you to accompany them to a business event or other activity, prepare to give your thirty-second elevator speech in a 10-second introduction of yourself, unless you have an opportunity to provide more in a later conversation.

Stacia Robinson, a franchise owner of BNI, one of the world's largest business networking organizations, says networking should be broken into two stages, "early networking" for new customers and "later networking" for prospects you've met before, and existing customers. She offers ten effective networking tips.

1. A one-page flyer. Have a brief overview of your business ready to pass along at all times.
2. Question-and-answer sheets. A sheet with questions and answers about your business could lead to a quick referral.
3. Testimonial letters from satisfied clients. Keep hard copies in a binder or post them to your website.

4. Photos of yourself, your office facilities, products, and awards. Photos of your office or business operation and products and awards help to legitimize your business and gain credibility.
5. Items that explain your business. These can include: your annual report, mission statement, news stories, or a written history of your company.
6. A list of your memberships and affiliations. This can be helpful when meeting someone for the first time, to see if you have mutual acquaintances or business associates.
7. Articles you have published or in which you're mentioned. Writing articles, or being mentioned in them, is a great way to become known as an expert in your field. People often prefer doing business with experts.
8. Client or customer proposals, bid sheets, or marketing letters. Having the ability to quickly refer to previously completed proposals may give you an edge with the prospect.
9. News reports on trends affecting your target market. Keeping up with issues and news items that are important to people can enable you to have targeted conversations with prospects.
10. New-product or service announcements. As you network, make sure the people who might potentially hire you or refer others to you are immediately informed when you offer new products or services or if you are expanding operations.

One final personal note, also be aware that exercising integrity is contagious. How you handle a situation can have a profound impact on those around you. I'm reminded of a personal story involving my children, who were about nine and twelve at the time. We were heading to the beach for a vacation and stopped at the drive-thru of a fast-food restaurant on the way. After receiving our food, I noticed the cashier had given me too much change. We had pulled away from the window and were about to get back on the road when I said, "We've got to go back." The kids protested because the line was long and they were anxious to get to the beach, but I returned the extra change. About a year later, it happened again when we were all together at another drive-thru and the cashier gave me too much change. This time, before I could say anything, my son blurted out with a deep sigh, "Oh man, let's go back, you know what we have to do." Sometimes, "more is caught than taught."[66]

THE REBEKAH PRINCIPLE

Once you've landed that new customer or client, the secret to building a long-term relationship is to create added value in the relationship. Remember, it's not about you or even your product or service. It's about your customer and what they want or need. Always be prepared to go above and beyond what the customer expects. My pastor recently delivered a message on "The Rebekah Principal." He spoke of how Rebekah's single act of giving generously, above what was expected blessed her tremendously and affected generations to come because it placed her in the bloodline of Jesus Christ. Her example is one by which we all need to live and conduct business. Rebekah's story is found in Genesis 24:12–19:

> **Genesis 24:12–15**
>
> *Then he prayed, "LORD, God of my master Abraham, make me successful today, and show kindness to my master Abraham. See, I am standing beside this spring, and the daughters of the townspeople are coming out to draw water. May it be that when I say to a young woman, 'Please let down your jar that I may have a drink,' and she says, 'Drink, and I'll water your camels too' – let her be the one you have chosen for your servant Isaac. By this I will know that you have shown kindness to my master." Before he had finished praying, Rebekah came out with her jar on her shoulder.*
>
> **Genesis 24:18–19**
>
> *Drink, my lord, she said, and quickly lowered the jar to her hands and gave him a drink. After she had given him a drink, she said, "I'll draw water for your camels too, until they have had enough to drink.*

INFORMATION IS THE NEW CURRENCY

Everything about Rebekah indicates she had a giving and cheerful spirit. This spirit resulted in her being blessed immensely.

This same spirit is the key for success in business. In fact, it could very well be the competitive advantage that keeps you ahead of the competition. Go that extra mile for your customers and clients. Give generously and create added value for them. Regardless of the type of business you are in, in this age of social media, if you do not have a marketing plan where you are touching your clients and customers through e-mail, Facebook, LinkedIn, Google+, YouTube, Pinterest, Instagram, etc., I can say earnestly, you are being left behind. One of the best ways to maintain a competitive edge as a small business is to provide your customers and prospects with great content and information on topics (related to your product or service) that affect their lives daily. In this economy, smart businesspeople and marketers will tell you that information is the new currency. The people you touch with free valuable, relevant information will remember you when it is time to buy. Once your potential customers and clients SEE the solution you provide and EXPERIENCE the value that comes from it, they will begin to trust you and ACT in your favor and pay what you ask to acquire what you have to offer. This is one of the most important lessons you can learn as an entrepreneur to generate recurring revenue.

POWER POINTS

- Integrity is the secret sauce for networking and building business relationships.
- Your reputation and your word are two of your most valuable assets.
- Success in business is about creating sustained value for your customers.
- Find a mentor.
- People don't care how much you know until they know how much you care.
- In this economy, information is the new currency. Share it to build relationships.
- Develop the relationship before asking your customer or client to buy.
- Customers who SEE and EXPERIENCE the value of information you freely provide will trust you and be motivated to ACT and buy from you.

Chapter 9

SELF-CONFIDENCE

I can do all things through Christ who strengthens me.

Philippians 4:13(NIV)

SECRET #9: SUCCESSFUL ENTREPRENEURS HAVE SELF-CONFIDENCE

Successful entrepreneurs believe in themselves and that the actions they take will lead to fruitful results. Self-confident people don't wait for things before they act on them, most often they operate from a proactive mindset. Self-confidence means being decisive, having the courage to take action, and having the boldness to lead, or respond assertively, when necessary. When others see that you believe in yourself, they begin to believe in you as well. Therein lies a key secret, which is: 100% of whether you <u>believe in yourself</u> is dependent upon *how you <u>feel about yourself</u> and <u>how you see yourself</u>*. That's why it is critical for you to be your own best friend. When you feel good about yourself and see yourself being successful, your thoughts and actions project positively into the things you do and to the people with whom you interact. The key to this, however, is understanding and knowing that you are a child of God who loves you unconditionally. That's why it's so vitally important that you have a spiritual foundation based on a personal relationship with your Heavenly Father, through Jesus Christ. Knowing that you are a child of the Risen Savior who is with you 24/7 gives you the capacity to feel good about yourself, all the time.

Will you always make perfect decisions as you step out in faith? No, but the point is having the willingness and courage to step out and make the decision in the first place. It is a key secret to success. Being self-confident will require you to step outside your comfort zone and eliminate self-limiting beliefs. The more you do that, the more you extend your comfort zone. That's where real growth happens and new ideas and creativity fill your mind. It's been said that success comes to you when you get good at managing opportunity. You must make the effort and you must step out. Stepping out is not always easy when you've been picked on, bruised, battered and crushed by the pounding of difficult circumstances. There are three decisions I made early in life, that I pass on now, which helped me stay focused on my goal of finding joy and success. First, I committed my life to Jesus Christ. Second, I decided to live my life in a way that would make a difference in other people's lives. Third, I would not let circumstances define who I was, what I could become or what I could accomplish.

The *7 Universal Steps for Success* which I discussed in the Introduction are also key ingredients for not only building your self-confidence, but turning it into an incredible asset to propel you to great heights of success. These steps, which have been used by some of this country's most successful people will have a multiplier effect on anything you set your mind, heart and hands to. They will empower your self-confidence as you utilize your gifts and talents beyond even what you thought was possible. Following these steps and this system will begin to transform your life *"now in this time."* They will prepare you for opportunities that will move you from your present circumstance to the abundance, joy and peace God has promised.

Step 1. Develop An Effective Prayer Life.

Step 2. Imagine And Commit To Your Success.

Step 3. Be Willing To Learn And Create Value For Others.

Step 4. Be Willing To Change.

Step 5. Be Willing To Implement Change.

Step 6. Be Self-Motivated

Step 7. Be Self-Confident.

Remember, you can grow in self-confidence and each of these steps can be "learned" by you and utilized effectively to grow your business to the next level just like many other high achievers have done.

ENCOURAGE YOURSELF

Sure it's easy to declare all these wonderful things about people who already are imbued with tons of self-confidence. But what about a person who is depressed, fearful, timid, or finds him or herself in a difficult situation? Where do they even start to gain the confidence they need to not only excel, but to simply get out of the rut they find themselves in? I'm glad you asked. This is exactly the situation King David found himself in after the Amalekites burned the city of Ziglag, where he was camped, and kidnapped all the women and children, including his two wives. In addition to the stress of his wives being taken, his followers wanted to stone him to death because they were not there to protect the women and children as they should have been. Talk about being distressed, under pressure and even fearful. But David gave us the example of what we must do when we feel boxed in and need a way out. In 1 Samuel 30:6 we find these words:

> *And David was greatly distressed; for the people spake of stoning him, because the soul of all the people was grieved, every man for his sons and for his daughters:* **but David encouraged himself in the Lord his God**.

David *"encouraged himself in the Lord his God"* and God took it from there, giving him the strength and courage to move beyond his circumstance and find victory in securing the return of the women and children under his care. That is exactly where you start. You start by encouraging yourself in the Lord your God. In the Psalms, David provides the example of what else we should do when a crisis occurs. We are to continually praise Him and demonstrate our faith in Him. This is how David found favor in the eyes of God (Psalms 56:3–4, 9–11; Psalms 59:16–17; Psalms 63:1–7). Pastor David Jeremiah has a wonderful series on the life of David entitled, "The Tender Warrior." His message entitled, "David's Deep Depression" was particularly uplifting for me when it came to dealing with the stress and strains of financial challenges and the rut I found myself in a few years ago.

If you have any doubt that God your Father will be there to love, guide, and protect you in every circumstance, no matter what it is, Romans 8:31–39 was written just for you. Read and meditate on it:

> *What, then, shall we say in response to these things? If God is for us, who can be against us? He who did not spare his own Son, but gave him up for us all – how will he not also, along with him, graciously give us all things? Who will bring any charge against those whom God has chosen? It is God who justifies. Who then is the one who condemns? No one. Christ Jesus who died – more than that, who was raised to life – is at the right hand of God and is also interceding for us. Who shall separate us from the love of Christ? Shall trouble or hardship or persecution*

or famine or nakedness or danger or sword? As it is written:

For your sake we face death all day long; We are considered as sheep to be slaughtered. No, in all these things we are more than conquerors through him who loved us. For I am convinced that neither death nor life, neither angels nor demons, neither the present nor the future, nor any powers, neither height nor depth, nor anything else in all creation, will be able to separate us from the love of God that is in Christ Jesus our Lord.

When Evander Holyfield, a former heavyweight boxing champion, got into the ring at age thirty-four with Mike Tyson, the heavyweight champion in 1996, not many people gave Holyfield much of a chance to win the fight, including me (though I was pulling for him). Odds-makers saw Holyfield as a huge underdog. I remember Holyfield had an inscription embroidered on his boxing robe which simply read: "Philippians 4:13"[67] I don't need to remind you that Holyfield won that fight. Holyfield did not let what pundits were saying about him damage his self-confidence. They said he was washed-up and too old, but he ignored it. That scripture gave Evander Holyfield the self-confidence in his God-given abilities, and to know that he would win that fight. It is the same power that gave David the self-confidence to know that he had the ability to slay Goliath. David knew the source of his strength was his Heavenly Father. The power of God's Word is also available to you.

What would New York Jets quarterback Tim Tebow be doing if he listened to all the critics who said he couldn't play in the NFL? When he was a home-schooled high-school student, people told him he couldn't play because he didn't go to a regular high school. Tim and his mother needed to move into an apartment in a neighboring county, which made him eligible to play for the local high school he wanted to play for. One of Tebow's highlights as a high-school athlete was finishing a game on a broken leg.[68] In college, he became the first underclassman to ever win the Heisman Trophy.[69] Today, not only is he playing in the NFL, but he was drafted in the first round by the Denver Broncos in the 2010 NFL Draft. By popular demand, Tim Tebow worked his way from being the third-string quarterback to being the starting quarterback of the Denver Broncos. His self-confidence and ability to inspire his teammates resulted in his teammates and fans calling for him to lead the team. My prediction is that Tim Tebow will be successful and a leader when and where ever he is given the opportunity to play.

When Tebow was with the Broncos they lost in the playoffs and didn't make it to the Super Bowl. However, do you think Tebow considers himself to be a failure because they did not make it? I think you know the answer. The Super Bowl is the world's definition of success. Sure it would have been nice for Tebow to lead his team there, but that was not God's plan for him. Real success is doing positive things to change people's lives and move them closer to Jesus Christ. During the off season, Tebow did just that. He helped change lives by using his celebrity status to lift up the name of Jesus Christ and raise millions of dollars for nonprofit agencies, fulfilling their missions to help the poor and those in need. God calls us to help *"the least of these"* (Matthew 25:45). Because the source of Tebow's confidence is Jesus Christ, he can forge ahead, fulfill God's purpose in his life, and not worry about what his critics have to say. You need that kind of confidence. With Jesus Christ as the real quarterback, you can have Tebow-like confidence because you know Christ never misses completing the pass and touchdowns will always be scored in your life.

As mentioned, my youngest brother, at age forty-seven became the oldest rookie to play for a professional basketball team. It certainly shocked me to see him on CNN's *Headline News*, but there he was, thinning hair and everything. Philippians 4:13 is a favorite scripture of many people, and if you suffer at all from a lack of self-confidence, this should become one you memorize and meditate on as well.

Study, planning, preparation, and a belief in your personal abilities are the keys to self-confidence. John Thompson grew up in the small town of Riviera Beach, Florida, and went to Florida A&M University, a small college in Tallahassee. He grew up to become head of one of the country's largest corporations, Symantec, maker of the Norton Anti-virus. As CEO, the company grew from $600 million to $6 billion in revenues and during his tenure, he was the only African American leading a major technology company. The company's position as one of the world's preeminent global companies is attributable directly to Thompson's vision and leadership. Had he not been confident in his abilities, I dare say he would not have become chairman and CEO of Symantec, and taken that company into the height of success it has today. After 10 years as CEO of Symantec, Thompson has moved on to become CEO of Virtual Instruments, another major technology company.[70]

PERSISTENCE PAYS

If you are seeking financing for your business from a bank or investors, be prepared to get some rejections. But don't let it shake your confidence. Keep your head up, keep your spirits high, and your confidence up. In the face of rejection, maintain a professional upbeat attitude. The confidence you demonstrate now may very well be what shows a bank official or investor that they need to reconsider. Don't approach a request for financing with a defeated or apologetic attitude. That attitude will come through in your conversation. Whenever you are turned down, don't beat yourself up. You will have plenty of naysayers ready to fill that role because they would love nothing more than to see you fail. Instead, focus your energy on the real reason they said no and adjust your approach for the next presentation. Even better, focus your creative skills on alternative routes, such as crowdfunding to obtain what you need. Remember, there is always another way, and oftentimes a better way. Barriers and insurmountable odds exist only in the minds of those who believe they exist.

Dr. A.G. Gaston, a prominent businessman I had the great fortune of knowing, was the pinnacle of persistence. In talking about the obstacles and rejections he often faced, he told me, it's not important how many times you get knocked down, what's important is how many times you get up. Dr. Gaston was known for saying, "Aside from sending His Son to earth, God's greatest gift to man was the power to think and overcome adversity."

Dr. Gaston was an African-American multimillionaire who was born into poverty in Demopolis, Alabama, in 1892. He later moved to Birmingham where he made his fortune. I met him in 1977, after receiving a partial scholarship from a fund he established at Samford University's Cumberland School of Law. He was eighty-five and still driving a Cadillac he had owned for several years. Of course driving was something his longtime executive assistant, Ms. Frierson, constantly attempted to persuade him to stop, but Dr. Gaston was undeterred. Dr. Gaston was 103 when he died in 1996. According to Wikipedia, his net worth was approximately $130,000,000. He enjoyed telling how he got started, but said he always had in his mind that he would not be poor all his life. He told me that it was really the funeral home business that moved his business career into "high gear." He worked at a steel mill in Fairfield, Alabama, at the time he began performing services for funerals. Work at the steel plant was hard, dangerous, and he earned less than $3.00 a day. When African-American workers died, they rarely had money for a funeral. He saw an opportunity and went around the community to collect money to bury his co-workers. He became known for being honest with the money he collected and providing the service of handling burials. Dr. Gaston told me he was always frugal with his money. He said, "I always paid myself a little first. This is my way of saving." He put off buying things for himself and ended up loaning money to co-workers, some of whom spent all they earned on the weekends. Of course, he charged interest on the money he loaned. The demand for his services grew in the community, which led to the formation of a funeral home company he co-owned called Smith and Gaston.

My sense was that Dr. Gaston felt poverty was an enemy that could be conquered, if the desire was present. He often referenced the "power of the mind" to accomplish great things. On one occasion, when we left his office at Citizens Federal Savings and Loan, he took me around Birmingham where we visited his funeral home business, a radio station he had recently acquired, the Gaston Motel, and Booker T. Washington Business College that was operated by his wife, Minnie, who was also an instructor. It was during this visit he told me, "Self-discipline is one of the greatest barriers to overcoming poverty, but knowledge and a mind to learn can fix that." Dr. Gaston did not let his early circumstances, station in life, or perceived obstacles deter him from the wealth and prosperity he believed he was entitled to enjoy. He felt that it was available to anyone with the determination to go after it. Dr. Gaston was truly a giver. His life and legacy demonstrate how persistence and his mental fortitude paid off. It enabled him to help thousands battle against poverty through the many educational opportunities, scholarships, nonprofit organizations, programs, and business endeavors he created.

As a side note, I did not know at the time of my visits with Dr. Gaston that part of the time I spent with him was a job interview. It was certainly a big confidence booster when he offered me my first job out of law school. I respectfully told him that business was my passion, but I felt called to a different area of work at that time. He understood and encouraged me to continue to pursue my dreams. I stayed in touch with him for many years until he passed away.

Self-confident people are diligent and persistent. They understand there will be setbacks, but they persist in spite of them. Thomas Edison, who invented the light bulb, phonograph, and more, faced setback after setback. Yet he never gave up on his endeavors. We benefit from Edison's persistence every day. On one occasion when asked how he felt about the thousands of unsuccessful attempts at getting a working light bulb, he said he viewed them as victories because he now knew thousands of ways of how *not* to perfect the light bulb.

Keep a positive attitude about yourself with Jesus Christ as the source of strength upon which you rely and your self-confidence will blossom. Your attitude has everything to do with your self-confidence. Be prepared for rejection, because it's going to happen. Don't take it personally and don't make it personal. Don't let the negative influences caused by doubt or rejection creep into your thinking. That's what your enemy Satan would have you do. He would have you believe that you don't deserve to be successful or that as a child of God, you can have wealth and be prosperous. But here's a secret. You can control what you think about. Second Corinthians 10:5 tells us to bring *"into captivity every thought to the obedience of Christ."* So if you are having a crisis of confidence, bring to mind a favorite scripture you've memorized. You'll feel your confidence being restored. I love the persistence and self-confidence of Jacob, who, as it is told in the Bible, wrestled with

God. When Jacob was told to let go of the "man" he was holding on to, even after his hip was wrenched, Jacob replied, "*I will not let go unless you bless me*" (see Genesis 32:26). Be like Jacob and be persistent until you achieve the goal you set for yourself.

In many cases, a lack of self-confidence goes back to one's childhood or self-limiting beliefs. It may come from negative comments of one's own parents or relatives. It could stem from so-called friends or from bullying by schoolmates. It could even come from insecurities about one's own looks or other perceived shortcomings. But know that all these things can be overcome. If you look around, you will find many people who have overcome major tragedies from their childhood. Christian Bible teacher and author Joyce Meyer is a great example of what God can do for a person's self-confidence. She often shares her story of being sexually abused as a child, and as a young adult was divorced from a cheating husband. But today Meyer has been named by *Time* magazine as one of America's Top 25 Most Influential Evangelists.[71] Her television and radio programs air in thirty-nine languages in two hundred countries, and she has written more than eighty books on Christianity.[72] Her book entitled *Battlefield of the Mind* was simply a game changer for me and it cut right to the heart of how Satan attacks your mind. This book makes it plain that Jesus Christ is the answer and response for every satanic attack and you can only protect your mind with the Word of God.

In addition to focusing on God's Word, find a godly friend, counselor or get involved in a Christ-centered church with active small groups where you can be around people whom you can share your feelings and find encouragement. I am blessed to serve at Church of the Highlands in Montgomery and to be among people who constantly encourage and pray for me. Likewise, I encourage and pray for them. We remind each other to always pray for and speak blessings over our nation, our leaders, our families and ourselves. Despite what may be going on in your life, seek to get to a place where you can begin to praise and honor God first. For example say: *"Thank you God for loving me. I praise You and honor Your Holy Name."* Next, pray for protection and God's favor on your family and others around you. Finally, pray for your own needs, what you want God to do for you, then claim it! As you pray in this way, you will see God move in your life to the point where your self-confidence grows steadily and your faith becomes stronger. Also read and recite the model prayer that Christ gave His disciples which can be found in Matthew 6:9-13, which reads:

> *"This, then is how you should pray: Our Father in heaven, hallowed be your name, your kingdom come, your will be done, on earth as it is in heaven. Give us today our daily bread. And forgive us our debts, as we also have forgiven our debtors. And lead us not into temptation, but deliver us from the evil one."*

ALWAYS REMEMBER THIS

If you don't remember anything else from your study in this book, remember it is critically important that you encourage yourself in the

Lord, <u>daily</u>. *Each night* before bed and when you rise *each morning* repeat these words: *"I am a child of God"* (John 1:12) *"I am free from condemnation"* (Romans 8: 1-2) ; I am *"strong in the Lord"* (Ephesians 6:10) *"I have been chosen and appointed to bear fruit"* (John 15:16); I can do all things through Christ who strengthens me. (Philippians 4:13 NJKV): By using the words "I am," "I can" and "I have been chosen," you are claiming and receiving, <u>in the here and now,</u> blessings, favor and protection God has for your life, including the ability to lead a prosperous and fruitful life for Him. There are many other scriptural words of encouragement you can locate and recite, but this daily exercise will transform your life beyond anything you can imagine. By speaking these words, you are declaring and becoming who God says you are and not what Satan would mislead you to believe. (See, Joshua 1:8 (NIV) This exercise is both offensive in moving you closer to God and defensive against the attacks of Satan that are designed to destroy your self-confidence. God promises that He will never leave you nor forsake you.[73] If God is for you who can be against you?[74] Satan does not want you to realize this, but everyday God gives you an opportunity to participate in His glorious plan for the world.[75] That means you are special to God. No one else can fulfill your purpose or do that which only you are called to do with the gifts and talents you may not have even begun to tap into. Your testimony and talents will bless and encourage many others. That's why God wants to bless and prosper you. All you have to do to claim your place is to believe, trust and allow Him to do His good work through you. Confidence in yourself will come simply because you are stepping out in the name of Jesus Christ.

Self-confidence is also equated with self-esteem or what you think about yourself. You should always think good thoughts about yourself. Speak blessings on yourself. Have an expectation that good things and blessings are going to come your way because you are a child of God. There are already enough people in the world ready to pounce and put you down for the slightest thing, no matter what you do. You've probably already run into a few of them. What sense does it make for you to help them destroy your self-esteem by giving in to their lies. It's like taking the bat out of their hands and banging it against your own head. Most often, their attacks are a cover-up for their own insecurities. Reject their lies, no matter who they are coming from. When Peter began to rebuke Christ for describing events to come, Christ rejected, as a lie, what Peter said and told him: "Get behind me, Satan! You are a stumbling block to me." You can reject the lies in the same way. The lies are designed to keep you away from God and steal your destiny of a blessed abundant life through Jesus Christ. John 10:10 says:

> *The thief does not come except to steal, and to kill, and to destroy. I have come that they may have life, and that they may have it more abundantly.*

Proverbs 23:7 (NKJV) says: *"For as he thinks in his heart, so is he."* Starting right now, bring uplifting thoughts about yourself to the forefront of your mind. It's not important what you may have done in the past, God has already forgiven you for it.[76] Christ is telling you to bring whatever is burdening you and leave it with Him, so that you can focus on being all the wonderful things He calls you to be.[77] That includes confronting your fears; controlling fears; and, conquering your fears.

When it comes to being an entrepreneur, self-esteem is everything. If you don't hold yourself in high regard, don't expect others to either. I'm not talking about being arrogant. There is a difference between self-confidence or self-esteem and arrogance. Self-confidence draws people to you. Arrogance does just the opposite. The main point here is that you must like yourself to be successful. Famed business coach and author Brian Tracy says that "self-concept" regulates every area of your success in sales. He says most "self-limiting concepts" are not real except to the extent you convince yourself they are real. Four additional points Tracy teaches his students are: 1) You become what you think about; 2) success breeds success; 3) the more you like yourself, the more you will earn; and 4) get up every morning, look in the mirror and say to yourself, "I like my self," "I like myself," "I like myself." If you add "I like myself" to the end of the scriptures in this section that you will recite each morning, nothing can hold you back and the world had better get ready! Thank you Lord!

POWER POINTS

- Memorize Philippians 4:13 (NJKV): *"I can do all things through Christ who strengthens me."*
- When you lack confidence, encourage yourself in the Lord.
- If God is for you, (and He is) nothing else matters.
- You really can do whatever you set your mind to.
- Don't take rejection personal. You are still a winner.
- Be persistent in the face of obstacles.
- Don't worry about haters and naysayers. They've got their own issues.
- Ask God to strengthen you in weak areas.
- Don't let the past define your future. You have been forgiven. It was preparation for this moment in time!
- You have a testimony and much to offer the world.
- Speak blessings on yourself and claim God's favor on your life.
- God wants you to participate in His plan for the world.
- Recite daily: "I'm a child of God!" – "I am strong in the Lord."
- How you feel about yourself has everything to do with how much you will earn in business.
- The better you feel about yourself, the more you will earn in business.
- Success is within your reach. God has your back.

PART VI.
BATTLE STATIONS!

I am aware that my enemy Satan is real and is engaged in spiritual warfare against me and my success as a believer in Jesus Christ. I understand that Satan's intent is to destroy me, my family and God's church. To fight this battle, I will praise and worship God daily and put on the full armor of God. I will use the spiritual weapons He provides to win the battle that include: the girdle of truth, the breastplate of righteousness, the gospel of peace, the shield of faith, the helmet of salvation, the sword of the Spirit which is the Word of God, and persistent prayer.

Reference:
Ephesians 6:10-18 (NIV)
Peter 5:8 (NJKV)
Isaiah 38:18-19 (NIV)

Chapter 10

GOOD HEALTH

Do you not know that your bodies are temples of the Holy Spirit, who is in you, whom you have received from God? You are not your own.

1 Corinthians 6:19 (NIV)

SECRET #10: SUCCESSFUL ENTREPRENEURS MAINTAIN GOOD HEALTH

An important part of climbing the ladder of success in business is being certain you are physically able to climb the ladder. Successful people know that they must remain vibrant and physically fit to face the rigors of operating a business. As people in business become consumed in dealing with the many challenges of the operation, they tend to overlook their own personal health and well-being, often putting in twelve- to fifteen-hour days, as well as time on the weekends. Their eating habits become terribly unhealthy. They fail to get enough sleep and don't exercise regularly. This is the perfect recipe for building up stress and having no place to release it. Your health and vitality are two of the most important gifts God has given you to fulfill your purpose and reach the goals of success. Like everything else you want to last, your health has to be nurtured and the proper attention given to it.

There are laws of nature that simply cannot be ignored when it comes to your health and physical fitness. One of those laws is the "law of becoming." Simply stated, as it relates to your physical health, the "law of becoming" is the change that takes place in your body, for better or worse, regardless of what you do. As you grow older, changes in your body occur whether you eat and exercise correctly or not. With each passing day, your body is "becoming" something. Whatever that "something" turns out to be, in many ways it is within your control. Three things that are within your control are diet, exercise, and an annual medical exam. Things you do not control are your family medical history (what you inherit) and things in your environment. The point here is to take charge of the things you have knowledge of and/or can control so that your quality of life is better in later years, and is better as you grow your business. Plant the seeds of a healthy diet and regular exercise in your life so you can reap the benefits of fighting off disease and ailments that come with a sedentary lifestyle. Studies show that heart disease, for the most part is preventable. For the sake of those who love you, commit to a healthier life style.

SILENT KILLERS

Stress, heart disease, and hypertension (high blood pressure) are three of your greatest enemies on your path to success. All three are literally silent killers that can have devastating effects on your physical and emotional well-being. Stress for example can adversely affect you in your personal and business relationships. It makes you irritable and short-tempered, and, what's worse, you may not even be aware of it. I can assure you, however, those around you will notice.

Both hypertension and heart disease left unchecked can be debilitating and will take you out of the game in the long run. Like any other enemy you face in life, you need God on the frontline to help you in battling these enemies. In order to take on the burdens of these enemies, you must carry it to God in prayer. In Matthew 11:28–30 (NIV):

> *Come to me, all you who are weary and burdened, and I will give you rest. Take my yoke upon you and learn from me, for I am gentle and humble in heart, and you will find rest for your souls. For my yoke is easy and my burden is light.*

The choice to maintain your bodily temple is up to you. Your personal physician is certainly where you want to make your first stop for advice. You honor God when you actively care for the body with which you have been blessed and where the Holy

Spirit dwells. Drs. Al and Terry Vester, a husband and wife team who operate the Vester Health Center in Lafayette, Alabama, say there are six things that are universally accepted for entrepreneurs and all others to do in seeking to maintain good health and vitality. They are:

1. Drink plenty of water.
2. Maintain a healthy diet with abundant nutrition.
3. Exercise regularly.
4. Get adequate sleep and rest.
5. Avoid smoking and excessive alcohol.
6. Get regular check-ups.

CHANGE OR DIE

Physical health is a big area that entrepreneurs often ignore. You heard it before: "If you don't change, you will die." How many times have you seen a bank vault connected to a U-Haul trailer following a hearse? How many people on their death beds proclaim, "I wish I had spent more time at work or at the office?" These comments have had little effect on getting people to change. When I served as president of the Montgomery Chapter of the American Heart Association, I received firsthand, many studies and reports that showed the "preventableness"[78] of most heart-related afflictions. The answer then is the same as it is today. Significant improvements can be made with changes in lifestyle that are in the hands of the individual patient. The real problem is people refuse to change their lifestyles. In fact, studies show that even in the face of certain death, most people are unwilling to change their lifestyles. Dr. Joe Furman, in his best-selling book *"Eat to Live"*, says:

> Heart disease is the number one killer in the United States, accounting for more than 40 percent of all deaths. Each year, approximately 1.25 million Americans suffer a heart attack or myocardial infraction (MI: more than 400,000 of them die as a result). Most of these deaths occur soon after the onset of symptoms and well before victims are admitted to a hospital. Every single one of those heart attacks is a preventable tragedy, as it could have been avoided.[79]

Another health-related leading cause of death that gets less attention but is related to heart disease, diabetes and other medical complications is obesity. A study released on January 4, 2013, by the AP-NORC Center for Public Affairs Research revealed that the U.S. public considers obesity to be second to cancer as the nation's most serious health issue, but AP quoting a New York Montefiore Medical Center dietitian, reported that people are often "shocked" to hear how far-reaching the effects of obesity are.[80]

The real question is why won't people change? For the answer, let's examine a fascinating series of landmark behavioral studies regarding the health crisis in the United States, starting with several reported in the May 2005 edition of *Fast Company*. The studies were presented at IBM's "Global Innovation Outlook" conference. The results are quite telling, but the recommendations suggest promise. The truth is that getting people to change is a far deeper challenge than most realize and even the prospect of death is not a strong enough motivator to get many people to change their behavior, over time.

The Studies

- Dr. Raphael "Ray" Levey, founder of the Global Medical Forum, told the audience "A relatively small percentage of the population consumes the vast majority of the healthcare budget for diseases that are very well-known and by and large behavioral." Dr. Levey says these people are sick because of how they choose to live their lives, not because of environmental or genetic factors beyond their control.
- Dr. Edward Miller, dean of the medical school and CEO of the hospital at Johns Hopkins University, said about 600,000 people have bypasses and 1.3 million have angioplasties at a cost of around $30 billion, annually, Dr. Miller said, "If you look at people after coronary-artery bypass grafting two years later, 90 percent of them have not changed their lifestyle and that's been studied over and over again. And so we're missing some link in there.

Even though they know they have a very bad disease and they know they should change their lifestyle, for whatever reason, they can't."

- John Kotter, a Harvard business school professor who has studied organizations in upheaval says, "The central issue is never strategy, structure, culture or systems. The core of the matter is always about changing the behavior of the people. He added: "Behavior change happens mostly by speaking to people's feelings."
- Dr. Dean Ornish, founder of the Preventative Medicine Research Institute, in Sausalito, California, says: "We also need to bring in the psychological, emotional, and spiritual dimensions that are so often ignored." Dr. Ornish persuaded Mutual of Omaha to pay for a trial study where researchers took 333 patients with severely clogged arteries and helped them quit smoking and go on Ornish's diet. The patients attended twice-weekly group support sessions led by a psychologist and took instruction in medication, relaxation, yoga, and aerobic exercise. The program lasted for only a year, but three years later, the study found 77 percent of the patients had stuck with their lifestyle changes and safely avoided the bypass surgery or angioplasty that they were eligible for under their insurance coverage. Mutual of Omaha saved about $30,000 per patient. Why does the Ornish Program succeed while the conventional approach failed? Dr. Ornish recast the reason for change. He says doctors had been trying to

motivate patients mainly with the fear of death and that simply wasn't working. For a few weeks after a heart attack, patients were scared enough to do whatever their doctors said. But death was just too frightening to think about, so their denial would return, and they'd go back to their old ways. Instead of trying to motivate them with the "fear of dying," Ornish reframes the issue. He inspires new vision of "the joy of living" –convincing them they can feel better, not just live longer. "Joy is a more powerful motivator than fear," he says. Reframing the issue alone is not enough, of course. Even when leaders have reframed the issues brilliantly, it's still vital to give people the multifaceted support they need. That's a big reason why 90 percent of heart patients can't change their lifestyles, but 77 percent of Ornish's patients could because he buttressed them with weekly support groups with other patients, as well as attention from dieticians, a psychologist, nurses, yoga, and medication instructors.

2012 Data

- In the next twenty years, more than 40 percent of the U.S. population is expected to have some form of cardiovascular disease, and this will triple the total direct medical costs of caring for hypertension, coronary heart disease, heart failure, stroke, and other forms of cardiovascular disease from the current $273 billion to more than $800

billion, according to a new policy statement from the American Heart Association (AHA).[81]
- In addition, the AHA estimates that the prevalence of cardiovascular disease will increase by approximately 10 percent over the next twenty years given no changes to prevention and treatment trends. If some risk factors, such as diabetes and obesity, continue to increase rapidly, cardiovascular disease prevalence and associated costs might increase even more, wrote Dr. Paul Heidenreich (Veteran Affairs Palo Alto Health Care System, California) and colleagues in the report, published online January 24, 2011, in *Circulation*.
- At present, cardiovascular disease is the leading cause of death in the U.S. and accounts for 17 percent of overall healthcare expenditures. In the past, the medical costs of cardiovascular disease increased at an average annual rate of 6 percent, and this growth in costs has been associated with an increase in life expectancy. That said, there are "many opportunities to further improve cardiovascular health while controlling costs," according to the AHA.

BUT WHAT CAN I DO?

The study performed by Dr. Ornish demonstrates that people <u>can</u> be taught to change their lifestyles for their benefit, by having weekly support groups that include attention from dieticians, a psychologist, nurses, yoga and meditation instructors. But that's not a realistic option for most of us unless your first name is Opra. The experts say, however there are things you can do to take back control of your life. It all begins with self discipline, but a good starting point is to get a check up and developing a long-term plan to improve and maintain your physical health. Learn about the benefits and consequences of eating certain foods. Learn about how ingesting more fiber in your diet will greatly improve the health of your digestive system.

There are some excellent support resources available to assist you in this area. All of them should be evaluated closely by you to be certain they are a good fit for you, including the ones I have referenced here in the book. Here are some to start with: Dr. Joel Furman's, book, *Eat To Live, with the sub-title "The Amazing Nutrient-Rich Program for Fast and Sustained Weight Loss."* This is a fascinating book that breaks down the truth about the American diet and how it's affecting your health. Two other highly sought after resources are Dr. Don Colbert's book, *The Seven Pillars of Health,* and Dr. Daniel Amen's book, entitled *Use Your Brain to Change Your Age.* Dr. Amen's new book is based on thirty years of brain-imaging research where he provides an interesting journey into how an informed healthier lifestyle can not only improve one's general health, it will also significantly improve the health of your brain and brain functionality. Many people have attested that Dr. Amen's program has helped them overcome depression, combat anxiety, increase energy, improve memory, and drop unwanted pounds. To help people get results,

Dr. Amen offers a free web-based and fee-based wellness program at http://theamensolution.com.

Physicians from various disciplines are beginning to also endorse different weight loss systems, but are going further and enrolling in the systems themselves. Dr. Mary Cassals, an endocrinologist and Dr. John Jernigan an internist with separate practices in Montgomery, Alabama, both subscribed to the Medifast system and recommend it to their patients. Dr. Cassals says: It's vital that patients understand that they truly are what they eat." Dr. Jernigan, who has lost more that 30 pounds on the Medifast system says: *"The best way to lead is by example. The other two doctors in my practice and most of my staff are now on the system. Not only has the weight loss among the staff been significant, the reliance on medications for various ailments, including myself has been reduced."* Dr. Jernigan and Dr. Cassals both say they like the support of this program, but the big feature that has made the difference is the individualized coaching that participants get. Patients are encouraged to stay on task and focused on their plans and progress between visits to the doctor.

There are many actions you can take to gain control of your health, starting with a visit to a physician for a checkup. Educate yourself about your own specific health concerns. Formulate a plan for adapting new habits for a healthy lifestyle. Get your family involved. Hang around healthy people. Through your church or among friends, organize a small group of people who like to walk or jog. They will encourage you to develop healthy habits. My mother told me she was once a smoker when I was very young.

She told me she quit smoking because she did not want her four children to become smokers. Her efforts worked and none of my siblings has ever been a smoker.

You must learn to think of your health as something you protect and nurture. It is something that provides you vitality your whole life through. On this path to success and prosperity, you must make maintaining good physical health a priority. After all, it's not just about you. It's also about those who love you, too.

POWER POINTS

- Your body is a temple of the Holy Spirit – protect it.
- You must maintain good health and vitality for success.
- You control what your body is "becoming." Plant the seeds of healthy habits.
- Stress, heart disease, and hypertension are silent killers. Get a checkup to live better and longer.
- Find a system and plan that works for you.
- Commit to a lifestyle for your health, not just a diet.
- Drink plenty of water, get adequate sleep and rest, and avoid smoking and excessive alcohol.
- Proper diet and exercise are keys to good health.
- Get your family involved in a healthy lifestyle.
- Join a support group.
- Count the joys of living a longer, healthier life.
- Live healthy for your love ones.

Chapter 11

STAY FOCUSED ON YOUR MISSION – MANAGE DISTRACTIONS

I press toward the mark for the prize of the high calling of God in Christ Jesus.

(Philippians 3:14)

SECRET #11: SUCCESSFUL ENTREPRENEURS MANAGE DISTRACTIONS

Successful entrepreneurs are not only able to stay focused on their missions, they manage distractions effectively. There is no way to predict every source from which you will encounter distractions. But know they are out there and they will surely come. The consequence of distractions is they knock you off course from your mission. They disrupt your thinking. Distractions will take over your life and cause you to forget about all the personal, business, and financial goals you have for yourself. You must be prepared to deal with them effectively. That does not mean you have to come up with the perfect response to every challenge you face, because you won't. But with Jesus Christ as your shield and anchor, you must develop the type of character and focus that will enable you to boldly continue your journey despite the distractions and challenges you will encounter. The key is to stay focused and manage them because "life happens." If you are not prepared to deal with them, you will find yourself consumed by them and sinking fast. My best advice is to follow the example set by Jesus. In Hebrews 12: 2–3 (NIV) we find these instructions:

> *Fixing our eyes on Jesus, the pioneer and perfecter of faith. For the joy set before him he endured the cross, scorning its shame, and sat down at the right hand of the throne of God. Consider him who endured such opposition from sinners, so that you will not grow weary and lose heart.*

DISTRACTIONS IN ACTION

Distractions can cause you to become indecisive, imprudent, and even gullible. Their purpose is to contribute to your defeat, give you a sense of hopelessness and create in you a victim's mindset. Distractions in most instances are difficult to identify because they come in all forms, shapes, sizes, people, places, and things. Distractions create stress and cause discouragement, disappointment, depression, physical illness, and divorce. If it causes you to take your eyes off God and forget or discard the personal goals for success you have set, you are going to need a course correction. Distractions can take the form of any of the following:

- business transactions that go bad
- a strained marital relationship
- job loss
- a failing business venture
- oppressive debt
- drug or alcohol abuse
- any sort of addiction (like online pornography or prescription drugs) or negative behavior
- an unexpected financial challenge
- problems at work
- difficulties with children
- problems with your health.

Distractions that keep you from achieving your goals and attaining the success you desire can also come in the form of things that are not necessarily bad. These things can cause an equally high level of frustration because they are not normally perceived as obstacles to success. They are just things that occur in life that are not factored in when we set our goals. These are things like:

- caring for aging or sick parents
- getting the kids to soccer or baseball practice
- recovering from an illness or surgery

- a job promotion with increased duties
- spending more time with your spouse and children
- getting kids through college.

The point here is to have an awareness that many factors can impact your goals and timetable. It is vitally important for you not to allow things that naturally occur in your everyday life to cause you to abandon your goals and aspirations to achieve success. It's about having the right attitude because life simply happens. Factor in these types of things when you set your goals and look for the joy in doing them. For example, we are told from the Ten Commandments to *"Honor thy father and thy mother: that thy days may be long upon the land which the LORD thy God giveth thee."*[82] We should always find joy in caring for aging parents who cared for us during our tender ages. Plus, it's what God tells us to do for our own benefit. Review and use the Anti-Mire Action Plan which I discussed in Chapter 2 and download the sample checklist from my website. It's a great way to bring the challenges to the forefront and put them in perspective so you can act appropriately on them.

COURSE CORRECTION

Because distractions are a part of life, managing them effectively must also become a part of your life. When distractions occur and take you off course from your plans, you need a course correction. Did you know once an airplane takes off and is in flight, it is off course 80 percent of the time en route to its destination? For most of us, taking a flight from Atlanta to Los Angeles is uneventful, as it should be. What you don't realize is that for 80 percent of the flight, you are off course. A retired Air Force chaplain I know often described in his sermons how the autopilot responded to outside forces that caused his plane to veer off course. He said the plane flies for a while and then checks to see if outside forces (*distractions*) have knocked it off course. If it has, the autopilot makes a course correction. As the flight continues, the autopilot performs another check and makes another course correction. This process continues until the plane lands safely at its destination. The ability to manage the distractions of life is no different when it comes to reaching the goals and destinations you've set for your life and your business. You don't change the destination, you engage the "autopilot" to put you back on course until you reach your destination.

Your "autopilot" is Jesus Christ. He has already paved the way and paid the price for you to successfully reach your destination. As soon as that first outside force hits, 1) take it to God in prayer; 2) lay out a plan to deal with it; and 3) stay focused on your ultimate goal. The more distractions you encounter, the more you pray and follow this process. Prayer should be your automatic reaction to obstacles. Trust in Him with all your heart and He will direct your path.

FINANCIAL DISTRACTIONS

I find that financial distractions and challenges in one's personal life often rank highest among distractions which require effective management. Very few of us have not felt the constant stinging pressure of debt, financial obligations, and the calls of heartless creditors at one time or another. It is critical to learn how to manage financial challenges so you won't be knocked off course and remain off course. So today, I am exposing financial distractions for what they are. They are tools of Satan designed to cause your defeat! But also today, this book will equip you with counter-measures. Spiritual counter-measures that come from the Word of God are defensive tools that prevent the torpedoes and fiery darts of Satan from destroying their intended targets, which in this case is you and me.

FINDING REAL HELP

The real question is: "Why do so many of us fail at gaining control of our personal finances?" The answer is simple. Most often, we attempt to undertake this great feat in our own strength. We don't look first to our Lord and Savior, Jesus Christ, for the strength to tackle the problem. I must admit that I thought I had it "going on" as I handled my finances. However, over the years, my income increased, but so did my debt and the stress that comes with it! My way was not working (that's the short version). After a few encounters of the not-so-pleasant kind, I decided that I needed to seek a peace that surpasses all understanding, which guards my heart and mind.[83] A peace that could only be given by Christ himself, and what a peace it was! I found great strength when I surrendered my burdens to Him. As I waited for a breakthrough, I continued to study His Word by starting each day with prayer and meditation. I continued to teach Sunday School, participate in small groups and remained active in church. Eventually, God took away the fear of losing my business, my home, and the material things I owned. He took away the fear of worrying about what people would think if I lost everything. God gave me a peace about my whole situation and what my life should really be about. He took me to a place where I can and will continually give Him praise despite what may be going on around me. In Romans 8:28, we find these words: *"And we know that in all things God works for the good of those who love him, who have been called according to his purpose."* I had to learn and understand that my existence in this world is not about me. Even if I lost everything, it would still serve His purpose. I had learn that nothing is too hard for God and He would meet my needs in any circumstance.[84]

More importantly, I had to learn that this was a spiritual battle as God's Word tells us in Ephesians 6:10–18. To fight a spiritual battle, I needed, as we all need, spiritual armor and spiritual weapons. I needed the "Full Armor of God." (Discussed in Chapter 12) I remain particularly thankful God sent me a wife of nearly thirty-two years now, who loves Him and puts Him first, too. When I explained the full extent of our financial situation to her, she was not a happy camper, to put it mildly. But if we had not turned to the Word of God together and allowed Him to comfort and direct us, the fiery financial darts Satan threw at us could have destroyed our marriage as they have unfortunately done to many. After we prayed together, we began to thank God that money was the only problem we had. We thanked Him that our children were doing very well, God had delivered our son through two life-threatening events, my parents were fine, we were in good health, and there were many other things to be thankful for.

The peace that God gave my wife and me took away the fear – and that peace is available to you. Turning to Jesus Christ and handing your situation over to Him is an essential first step on the journey to real freedom, prosperity, financial independence, and ultimate success. Consider this verse: *"Peace I leave with you, My peace I give to you; not as the world gives do I give to you. Let not your heart be troubled, neither let it be afraid"* (John 14:27–28).

THE DEBT AND TAX BUG BIT ME, TOO

Three of the biggest mistakes I made early in my career was 1) not having an appreciation of how pervasively debt controls your life, 2) not paying cash to avoid debt (paying cash requires saving), and 3) not having a realistic plan to eliminate the debt I had. I was blind to a simple basic principle that wealthy people live by. That is: "When you eliminate debt, you automatically create wealth that moves you toward financial independence." I rationalized having the debt by saying that I would one day make enough money and just pay it off. Despite the fact that I am in a profession where some people make lots of money, this strategy was no better than trying to hit the lottery. But no matter the profession or vocation, too many people spend excessively and create debt with the faint hope that "something" will happen in the future to bail them out. Sadly, for most, that "something" never happens. If you don't remember anything else from this chapter, remember this: *Expenses left unattended will always rise to the level of your income, like a thief in the night, robbing you of the financial freedom to control your own life and that of your family.* George S. Clason, author of the best-selling book, *The Richest Man in Babylon,* puts it this way, "That which each of us calls 'necessary expenses' will always grow to equal our incomes, unless we <u>protest</u> to the contrary." In 2007, my personal income was into seven figures. However, because I had not paid enough in estimated taxes to offset the increase in my income, I found myself negotiating an installment agreement with the IRS to pay taxes and had a tax lien placed on my home. I also did not have a serious and continuous debt-elimination plan and much of the debt I intended to pay off, lingered, including a couple of bank loans from business investments that came due and I was unable to pay them. I had to regonetiate new terms for both bank notes.

About that time, it had already hit me that I had to not only "talk the talk," I had to "walk the walk." I knew these were the kinds of things I had counselled others about. I also knew from experience that the overwhelming majority of small-business owners face financial challenges at some point in their growth and development. Because I was embarking on a new career as a business coach and consultant and beginning to write books to help small businesses, I now had to take my own advice. I had to be strategic and intentional about embarking on a plan to eliminate my debt and reduce my tax liability. It was not good enough to take a hit-and-miss approach. I had to "protest" (avoid) new debt, some of which I considered a "necessary expense," such as replacing my 10-year old car with a new one. My car is paid for and is in good condition. But then

I asked myself why I should become an indentured servant to a bank for four or five more years just for that new car smell when saving that $60,000 over the life of the note will put me closer to being debt free with real financial independence? I could be paying myself (saving) or eliminating other debt with that money, which in either case, is creating wealth. I still have my car of ten years.

In 2008, I felt a calling to write this book and had already started down the path of becoming a full-time business coach and consultant focusing on helping small-business owners which I had had success in doing and enjoyed the work. I was taking very few new cases as a lawyer while looking for the right time to transition fully into my new profession, despite having made a very good living practicing law. My timing was not the best, but waiting for "the right time" is always an excuse not to take action when faced with fear of the unknown that includes the potential of financial calamity. I had counselled many other business owners through various financial crises and prayed with some of them about not being fearful. I must admit that counselling is a lot easier to do when the economics of the situation is not about you. I could have gone back and taken on more cases or taken a position with one of the firms I considered joining, but I chose not to do that. Instead, I stayed focused on my mission, began to manage the distractions and stepped out on faith. What I can tell you is that each time my situation appeared the darkest, God placed a "ram" in the bush for me. The "ram" may not have been there in the time I wanted it, but it was always there and it was always on time. It is a very interesting dynamic when your personal financial circumstances are "tight," but everyone thinks you're on top of the world. I was able to smile and persevere because I knew God had my back. I also know that God wanted me to grow while I was in that season. I think about so many others who are smiling on the outside, but are in turmoil on the inside. Their lives are like ticking time bombs waiting to explode. They can't see their way out of their situation and don't know where to turn. But that's where knowing and having faith in Jesus Christ would save and deliver me. He is available to you in the same way. Christ is inviting you to bring those burdens to Him whether they are financial, about relationships, children, your health, your business or job. He wants it all. I referenced this scripture earlier, but it brings me such comfort and peace that it bears repeating. In Matthew 28–30 (NIV), God's inspired Word says:

> *Come to me, all you who are weary and burdened, and I will give you rest. Take my yoke upon you and learn from me, for I am gentle and humble in heart, and you will find rest for your souls. For my yoke is easy and my burden is light.*

Try Him. That's my advice to you right now. Try Him. Sometimes the fear is so great, you become paralyzed and don't want to move. But that's when He wants you most. Your back is against the wall anyway, so why not try Him? I've heard this phrase said in different ways, but the essence of the phrase is this: : "*It's not faith if you have to see it to believe it. With faith, you have to believe it to see it.*" After years of abundance, things around our household got tight. But the tighter things got, the more I prayed. I continued to tithe, teach Sunday School, participate in church small groups, and attend Bible study. The more I worked on this book, the more satanic distractions popped up. Some were pretty intense. There were different choices I could have made, but because Jesus Christ was the anchor for both my wife and me, I was able to stay focused on my mission, manage the distractions, and have faith that He would carry me through it all. The publication of this book is my testimony that God has and continues to deliver me. But even more important is the fact that He can and will deliver you too. How is it that I can be so confident about your deliverance and success as well as mine? It's because you and I have a loving Heavenly Father who rejoices in our victories just as our natural fathers and mothers experience great joy in our accomplishments. Consider the words found in Zephaniah 3:17 (NKJV):

> "The Lord your God in your midst,
> The Mighty One, will save;
> He will rejoice over you with gladness,
> He will quiet you with His love,
> He will rejoice over you with singing."

TERRY'S TEN-STEP PLAN TO FINANCIAL FREEDOM

The ten-step plan below is what I am following to become debt free in five years:

1. I dusted off and revised the family budget with my wife, and did the same for my business. My favorite quote on this topic comes from John Maxwell: "Budgeting is telling your money where to go rather than asking it where it went."
2. I reactivated my savings plan and maintain an emergency fund.
3. I paid off smaller credit-card debt and destroyed the cards. I only have American Express which I use for travel, and a check card. (Dilemma: Available unused capacity on credit cards can have a positive effect on your credit score, so give this careful study before closing your accounts, even if you cut up the cards. Exercise self-discipline and do not give yourself an excuse to run them up again.
4. I negotiated with credit card companies to eliminate old debt with outrageous interest rates. I had made cash advances in years past when business was slow. In one case, a credit card company accepted 50 percent of the balance, which I paid over several months. Be aware, however, that when a credit card company forgives all or part of a debt, this is *income* to you on which you must pay taxes, unless you are insolvent. Can you believe that? It's true. The credit card company will send you a Form 1099-C and you'll need to complete a Form 982 so Uncle Sam can get his share of the forgiven debt. The key point here is to talk with an accountant or knowledgeable tax preparer whenever you have any debt forgiven.

5. I restructured my business debt to get favorable payment terms, including a reduced balance for early lump sum payoff. I am accelerating pay down of debt at every opportunity and I'm completing my installment plan payments to Uncle Sam.
6. I started paying cash for things. This eliminates unnecessary purchases and occasional impulse buying. (I like gadgets.)
7. We eliminated Direct TV, premium cable service and reduced the times we dine out.
8. I avoid new credit cards and creating debt like the plague. Remember Proverbs 22:7 says: *"Rich people rule over those who are poor. Borrowers are slaves to lenders."*
9. I am utilizing wealth-building strategies to increase my income, acquire assets, and reduce my federal income tax liability.
10. I am continuing to tithe and give at least 10 percent back to God – off the top. Plus, I am budgeting to give 10 percent or more of my business revenue back to God as well. Becoming debt free creates the financial freedom that allows your resources to flow more abundantly so you can cheerfully give more to God to be used for His purposes. Acts 20:35 (MSG) says: *"You'll not likely go wrong here if you keep remembering that our Master said, 'You're far happier giving than getting.'"*

Robert G. Allen, the author of the best-selling book, *Nothing Down,* who has made millions as an entrepreneur, will tell you very quickly that you have to give back to God "off the top." Of course, he will also tell you he learned that lesson after losing millions, having to file for bankruptcy, and then rebounding to his present status.

Because Jesus Christ is my rock, I can maintain a positive, hope-filled, and expectant attitude on this journey to financial independence and success, whether the journey takes me down in a valley or to a mountain top. My success and salvation are assured and yours is, too! Proverbs 2:7 (NIV) tells us: *"He holds success in store for the upright, he is a shield to those whose walk is blameless."*

THE MILLIONAIRE MINDSET

Millionaires think differently from most people. Millionaires understand that it's not how much money you earn that makes you a millionaire. It's how much you are able to keep. They will tell you that if you have heavy debt, you are nothing more than a conduit for those to whom you are indebted. The millionaire mindset understands why it's important for the entrepreneur to know the difference between an asset and a liability. People with the millionaire mindset acquire assets because assets work for them and put money in their pockets. Uninformed people, with a poor person's mindset acquire liabilities, which takes money out of their pockets.

The millionaire mindset also understands the critical practice of saving and paying cash for things. This mindset says that when you save, you are paying yourself. When you put the money in a savings account, you earn interest and now have an "asset" that is putting money in your pocket. Will you get rich overnight with a regular savings account? No, but you are actually disciplining yourself not to pour wealth into a liability or something that is not putting money in your pocket. Although interest rates on savings accounts are relatively low these days, it will benefit you tremendously to read a few articles on "compound interest."

Having the goal to live a debt-free life is attainable and within your grasp. However, it requires more than just declaring that you will live within your means. It requires preparation to fight an ongoing inner struggle to resist urges for things that bring you immediate temporary pleasure. Delayed gratification is the biggest secret to building wealth and becoming financially independent. It requires saving until you can pay cash for things you need or even desire. It requires putting extra income toward eliminating credit card and other debt. It requires a thoughtful approach to managing your finances, including preparing for retirement. Most of all, becoming debt free and financially independent requires you to exhibit Christ like qualities of patience and self-control as found among the *"the fruit of the spirit"* in Galatians 5:22–23.

> *But the fruit of the Spirit is love, joy, peace,* **forbearance,** *kindness, goodness, faithfulness, gentleness and* **self-control.** *Against such things there is no law.*

This was exactly the approach taken by two good friends, Ken and Annetta, who just completed building their "dream home." Ken is retired military and works for a company in the budgeting and finance department. Annetta works for a bank and they have put two boys through college. Ken describes himself and his family as regular people from very humble beginnings who have been blessed by God. They will tell you that planning is what has enabled them to build their new home despite the difficult economy. In their own words, here is how they did it.

CASE STUDY

How We Got Out of Debt and Stayed Out – You Can, Too!
By: Ken and Anetta Scott

2 Kings 4:7: "Then she came and told the man of God. And he said, 'Go, sell the oil and pay your debt; and you and your sons live on the rest.'"

We have learned over the years, that the above scripture tells us how to handle our finances. This is God's way. Any other way is man's way and quite frankly, man's way will ultimately fail. Most of us cannot pay cash for a home or a car; however, we can focus on paying off our debts early rather than continually racking up debt for material things.

When we were married in 1979, we accumulated approximately six credit cards – when we might have had really good credit after we graduated from college. In essence, we really didn't have any credit at all and like most other graduates, we received an endless supply of credit cards. When you opened your wallet and several credit cards were in view, you really felt proud. Well, that very thing happened to us. Little did we know at the time, but soon learned, this is not God's way.

Here are five simple tips to put into practice with 2 Kings 4:7 as your mental focus, you, too, can live a debt-free life:

1. Credit card debt is financial suicide. While paying bills one day, we noticed we had less than $100 left for food, clothing, etc. Guess where we pulled the needed funds from – the credit cards. We were in a cycle. We decided to pay them off one by one by giving postdated checks to some of the creditors (not sure if anyone accepts them now). Once the final payment was made, we cut the cards in half while we were still in the stores. We have changed our attitude about credit cards. If we charge now, we pay off before the end of the month. As a matter of fact we primarily put everything on one credit card. In addition, a record is kept of each transaction in a log divided into categories. At the end of the month, we can see what was spent in each category; namely, gas, clothing, what we shared with others, etc. Annetta does have a department store credit card in her name only. There is no running balance. "Charge and pay" within the grace period is our new motto.

2. One of us pays the bills – the other one saves. I am the primary breadwinner. For the last five or six years, Annetta saves her paychecks. We only used her income if there was tuition for our two sons while attending college approximately

six years ago, or when the IRS decided we didn't pay enough taxes. We tapped into our emergency fund.

3. Pay Tithes. For a long time, we only gave $25 or so in church, no matter how many times the Minister spoke about tithing. After we began to be more serious about our spiritual life, we began to prioritize which meant putting God first. This included giving Him what He requires (10 percent of our earnings). We were sowing seeds by being more intentional with tithing more of our earnings, then one day it hit us. We began to receive blessing after blessing. Now we sow a little more than $1,000 per month no matter what season we find ourselves in. God has seen us through our up-and-down seasons.

4. Car Note. We paid off $15,000 in one year for an auto loan. Annetta was losing her job due to a bank merger and we only wanted to have a mortgage and utilities. We used the same principle we used previously to get out of debt. To get that car paid off, we made payments of any extra cash we got our hands on. Our payments were all over the place and the amounts included payments of $8.00, $1,000.00, $550, and $12.00. When our sons asked Annetta what she wanted for her birthday, Christmas, etc., she replied, "money." When she received $200.00 as a gift from them, she would add an additional $350 or so and made the regularly scheduled payments. Remember the formula for a simple interest loan is principal x interest/365 x thirty days + the monthly interest.

We were paying $2.05 per day on $15,000 at 5.00 percent. Cutting down on the number of days between payments = paying it off early. The automated touchtone telephone service allowed me to make any payment amount 24-hours-a-day.

5. Retirement. We each take advantage of the 401-K plan offered by our employers. This is free money. Our employers match our contributions.

Finally, as a result of putting the above tips into practice and being intentional and committed, God enabled us to begin building our dream home in 2011. It is now completed and we are enjoying God's blessing!

****

What Ken and Annetta have done is an example of what financial guru Dave Ramsey often says: "Live your life like no one else, so that later, you can live your life like no one else."

POWER POINTS

- Stay focused on your mission and goals.
- Know that distractions are a part of life and can come from anywhere.
- Delayed gratification is the biggest secret to building wealth, becoming financially independent, and reaching your goals.
- Start each day with prayer asking God to give you the strength to effectively manage all distractions that come.
- Financial distractions are leading causes of failure and divorce. A closer relationship with Jesus Christ can fix both.
- Develop a financial plan to become debt free.

Chapter 12

PREPARED FOR SPIRITUAL WARFARE

Finally, my brethren, be strong in the Lord and in the power of His might. Put on the whole armor of God, that you may be able to stand against the wiles of the devil. For we do not wrestle against flesh and blood, but against principalities, against powers, against the rulers of the darkness of this age, against spiritual hosts of wickedness in the heavenly places.

Ephesians 6:10–12 (NKJV)

SECRET #12: SUCCESSFUL PEOPLE ARE PREPARED FOR SPIRITUAL WARFARE

The road to success is paved with dangers and challenges you must face, most often every day. As important as anything you've read in this book is to know that you have an enemy, Satan, who does not want to see you succeed and will do everything he can to derail your plans and destroy you in the process. Many of us don't even realize that there is a spiritual war going on against us. As a consequence, we are easily knocked off course, distracted and discouraged. Businesses fail, families are wrecked, and individuals vow never to aspire to do anything else because of their discouragement and disappointment. Our natural reaction when difficulties come is to try and fight these battles in our own strength or to turn to unhealthy practices such as illegal drugs, prescription medication, alcohol or even an illicit relationship. But as the scripture above tells us, our battle is not against flesh and blood, but against *"forces of evil in the heavenly realms."* As an entrepreneur, on this journey to success, you must be <u>aware</u> that this battle and warfare being waged against you is being fought out in the "heavenly realms" and in your mind. The blessing, however, is that God's Word prepares you for the battle of spiritual warfare you will encounter. The warfare you will face won't come at set times or with an appointment. In addition, the battle will be a daily one, which is why you must equip yourself daily with the full armor of God. The secret to successfully fight this battle continues through Ephesians 6:13-18, (NKJV).

> *Stand therefore, having girded your waist with truth, having put on the breastplate of righteousness, and having shod your feet with the preparation of the gospel of peace; above all, taking the shield of faith with which you will be able to quench all the fiery darts of the wicked one. And take the helmet of salvation, and the sword of the Spirit, which is the*

word of God; praying always with all prayer and supplication in the Spirit, being watchful to this end with all perseverance and supplication for all the saints –

Satan knows where your weaknesses are and throws darts where you are weakest. He does this to cause the following things to happen to you: 1) It takes your focus off your God who loves and cares for you, 2) It causes you to lose focus of your goals, mission and purpose in life, and 3) It causes you to make bad unhealthy choices that will lead to your destruction all because you are a believer in Jesus Christ.

In Ephesians 6:16, we find these encouraging words: *"Above all, taking the shield of faith, with which you will be able to quench all the fiery darts of the wicked one."* Note the word "all." This means that you cannot go to God and say: "But you don't understand *my* situation." God's Word in this scripture is telling you that "all" means "all." That no matter how big the problem, or the type of circumstance or "fiery dart," nothing is too big for God to handle.

The obstacles and challenges Satan uses are tools designed to control your mind and create fear and anxiety in your life. Satan wants to destroy your testimony, your household and your business. He even wants to discourage those even thinking about starting a business because starting a business is the fastest way to generate wealth and independence when done properly. The discouragements, disappointments, debt, and depression that you face are designed to rob you of your energy and your ability to focus and be successful in your business and personal life. The more you think about the distractions, the larger and worse the circumstances seem to become. That's when you need to call to mind a scripture you have memorized such as: *"God did not give us a spirit of fear, but of sound mind through Christ Jesus"* (2 Timothy 1:7").

When you constantly bring scriptures to mind, you are doing four very important things: First, you are no longer focusing on how big your problems are, you are now focusing on how big God is. Second, you are allowing God to remove the anxiety Satan has created in your mind by worrying and constantly thinking about your circumstances. Third, you are allowing God to give you peace that surpasses all understanding, in the midst of a difficult situation so that you can think rationally even though the pressure is on. Finally, and most importantly, you are taking control of what you think about and not allowing yourself to be a victim of the negative influences, and circumstances that cause you to doubt yourself and God's promises. This secret is at the heart of what will propel you to success in business and allow God to fight your battles for you. God's instructions are a covering regarding every thought that comes into our minds to prepare us as He says:

> *Casting down arguments, and every high thing that exalts itself against the knowledge of God, and bringing into captivity every thought to the obedience of Christ* (2 Corinthians 10:5 NKJV).

> *For as he thinks in his heart, so is he.* (Proverbs 23:7 NKJV)

In order to be prepared, it is important to think *about what you think about*. Know that Satan wants to control your thoughts to make you an ineffective influence for Christ. At the same time, he does not want you to even be aware that he is having such a divesting impact on your life. That's why it's vital to pray and keep on the full armor of God. When the attacks get particularly personal, (and sometimes they will) Psalms 56:8-13 (NIV) reminds me of God's protection and deliverance:

> *Record my misery; list my tears on your scroll – are they not in your record? Then my enemies will turn back when I call for help. By this I will know that God is for me. In God, whose word I praise, in the* LORD, *whose word I praise – in God I trust and am not afraid. What can man do to me? I am under vows to you, my God; I will present my thank offerings to you. For you have delivered me from death and my feet from stumbling, that I may walk before God in the light of life.*

MAKE JOY YOUR WEAPON OF CHOICE

As a young boy, whenever my grandmother Eula saw that I was disappointed about something, she would tell me, "*Don't let the devil steal your joy.*" At the time I really didn't understand what she meant. But as I grew older and studied God's Word more closely, I became astounded as to how much godly wisdom is packed in that simple phrase. I learned early that satan is real and his purpose is to destroy my life and the lives of every believer. 1 Peter 5:8 (NJKV) tells us: *Be sober, be vigilant; because your adversary the devil, as a roaring lion, walks about, seeking whom he may devour.* I came to understand that joy is a gift and a weapon that God has made available to us to battle the darts Satan throws to destroy us. As Christians, we are commanded to constantly seek the joy of the Lord so that we are always armed against the attacks of satan. Philippians 4:4 provides this: *"Rejoice in the Lord always: and again I say, Rejoice."*

Joy is strength like no other that enables each of us to endure the most trying of circumstances and to bear those things that are unbearable. It is evidence of our faith and of God's presence in our lives. When you have lost a loved one, joy is the assurance you have that your loved one is with God and you will be reunited with them again. When your body is filled with pain, joy is the strength, power and love of God within you that provides you comfort and peace in the midst of your suffering as you continually give Him praise. Nehemiah 8:10 says: *"The joy of the Lord is your strength."* Joy also has healing power as Proverbs 17:22 (NIV) says: *"A merry heart does good, like medicine, But a broken spirit dries the bones.* "When you are faced financial calamity in your business or personal finances you don't become frantic. Instead, you look to Him with an attitude of gratitude, receive His peace and face each situation knowing that you will learn from them and become a stronger person to fulfill His purpose for your life. *"Consider it pure joy, my brothers and sisters, whenever you face trials of many kinds, because you know that the testing of your faith produces perseverance"* (James 1:2–3, NIV).

WORRY IS A LACK OF FAITH

Worry is also a dart and distraction of the enemy that steals valuable time and energy you need to focus on important things that will make your business a success. In Matthew 6:27, the question is asked: "Can any one of you by worrying add a single hour to your life?"

Here is where you must exercise your faith and take the distraction, burden, and worry to Christ. When you find yourself worrying excessively about something, or unable to sleep at night, locate a scripture and memorize it. Each time the worrying thought comes to your mind, speak silently to yourself the scripture you've memorized. Here are two verses I memorized long ago and have mentioned in previous chapters. I bring them to mind in times when I struggle with worry:

- *"Trust in the Lord with all thine heart. Lean not unto thine own understanding."*[85]
- *"I can do all things through Christ who strengthens me."*[86]

Understand that there is a difference between "worry" and "concern." Worry is a self-destructive behavior that unnecessarily causes you to become discouraged, depressed, anxious, and distracted from your godly mission and goals. Worry is a lack of faith and will stop you dead in your tracts from accomplishing the plans God has to prosper you and care for you. Worry also can take a physical toll on your health. Philippians 4:6 tells us exactly what to do if we're ever worried:

"Be anxious for nothing, but in everything by prayer and supplication, with thanksgiving, let your requests be made known to God."

Concern, on the other hand, is an acknowledgment that there are circumstances, events and challenges for which you must plan and take action on with God as your guide. With concern, you are taking steps forward daily and continuing the journey toward the goals you have set for your life. You are not sitting around worrying and waiting for the sky to fall. You are taking steps to get back into God's will and get your life back on track, even if you are taking baby steps. With concern, you are always moving forward. Worry, on the other hand has a paralyzing and debilitating effect on your overall wellbeing. Worry is a tool of satan we are instructed by God to resist. James 4:7 says: *"Submit yourselves, then, to God. Resist the devil, and he will flee from you."*

In order to effectively manage the worries, pressures and distractions that come into your life, you must release them to God in prayer. Study His Word. Meditate on His Word. Let His Word penetrate your thoughts and mind. You will find that God's Word will give you peace in the midst of your distracting circumstance. Let God reveal to you a plan to walk you through the circumstance you are in. He may show you the situation could be as simple as better management of your time or discussing it with a godly friend.

BEYOND WHERE YOU THOUGHT YOU COULD GO

What we do know is that Jesus Christ does not want you to deal with your burdens alone. In Matthew 11:28–30, he instructs us to: "*Come unto me, all ye that labor and are heavy laden, and I will give you rest. Take my yoke upon you, and learn of me; for I am meek and lowly in heart: and ye shall find rest unto your souls. For my yoke is easy, and my burden is light.*" Handling difficult challenges in business when the warfare gets intense is easier said than done. But to have someone who is asking you to turn those burdens over to Him, as Christ invites you to do is an awesome notion. It is actually cause for celebration, to already know that you will come out victorious on the other side of whatever it is you are facing. Understanding this principle actually strengthens your faith in the things you hope for and in the things He gives you confidence to accomplish.

I heard Bishop T.D. Jakes preach a sermon called "Living Beyond Walls," which was about what you do when God does not answer that prayer in the time you think he should. In this circumstance, for instance, you don't get that bill paid in time or the house is foreclosed on. So what do you do? The answer is: You praise Him "anyhow." Do you remember the story of the Hebrew boys, Hananiah, Mishael and Azariah (most often referred to by their slave given names Shadrach, Meshach and Abednego) who were told if they continue to refuse to bow down to the king, they would be thrown in the fiery furnace and killed? Their response is an amazing example of the level of faith and conviction we must strive toward when facing fearful circumstances that can cause great pain or physical harm. Their response, found in Daniel 3:16–18, was, "*If it be so, our God whom we serve is able to deliver us from the furnace of blazing fire; and He will deliver us out of your hand, O* *king. <u>But even if He does not, let it be known to you, O king, that we are not going to serve your gods or worship the golden image that you have set up</u>.*"

Wow! Hananiah, Mishael and Azariah were unwavering in their commitment to God and did not allow their individual circumstances or pressure to conform to the world's standards to move or influence them. Of course we know God protected and delivered them from the furnace.[87] That's because they were in a place beyond where the king thought they could go. A place beyond fear and the king's threats. They were totally consumed in their faith to God. This is the place each of us must strive to reach. It represents the type of mindset we must have in dealing with the challenges we face each day. Your task each day, as is mine, is to put on the shield of faith along with the rest of God's armor in the same manner as Daniel's three friends did. Once that's done, you can handle "all" the fiery darts Satan will throw at you, no matter the threat. Moreover, you will be able to keep your focus on God's saving grace, your mission and purpose in life as you achieve the goals you've set for the success of your business.

POWER POINTS

- Understand that spiritual warfare is being waged against you by your enemy, Satan.
- Put on the "Full Armor of God" daily.
- Be aware that the battlefield is in your mind.
- Know that the struggle is daily and you must prepare daily.
- Keep your mind focused on Jesus Christ and things that are good. For as a person thinks, so is he.
- Put on the shield of faith so you can deflect *all* the darts that Satan throws to destroy you.
- Make joy and faith your weapon of choice. Joy provides inner strength.
- Give God praise and worship, no matter the circumstance.

PART VII.
WHAT'S REALLY IMPORTANT

I have faith in God because I know that without faith, it is impossible to please God. I will trust in God and follow His commandments. He will bless and provide for me. I will study and proclaim the Gospel for it is the power of God. I will find joy in sharing it with others because the Gospel offers the gift of Jesus Christ, who can heal all their sufferings and is the way to salvation.

Reference:
Hebrews 11:6 (NIV)
Proverbs 3:5-6 (NIV)
Ecclesiastes 12:13 (NIV)
Deuteronomy 30:16 (NIV)
Romans 1:16-17 (NIV)
Matthew 28:19 (NIV)

Chapter 13

EFFECTIVE TIME MANAGEMENT

Seek the LORD while he may be found; call on him while he is near.

(Isaiah 55:6, NIV)

SECRET #13: SUCCESSFUL ENTREPRENEURS MANAGE TIME EFFECTIVELY

NO TIME LIKE THE PRESENT

The Bible is God's time-management system for how to live a fruitful life on earth. God made time. Time is a non-renewable resource. Once it's gone, it's gone! You can never get it back. The amount of time each of us has on this earth is finite. James 14:4 (NIV) says, *"Why, you do not even know what will happen tomorrow. What is your life? You are a mist that appears for a little while and then vanishes."* Seeking the Lord in the time He has given, which is now, is an effective aspect of time management. Psalm 90:12 says *"Teach us to number our days that we may gain a heart of wisdom.*

I read recently a study that said life expectancy in the United States is about 80 years and that the average person only has approximately 29,000 days on this earth." When viewed in the context of the number of days, this information should provide a profound and enlightening perspective because the number of days for all of us is getting smaller. In other words, our time here is running out and the time is now for getting priorities straight. To make the most of the days you have remaining, the number one priority should be to seek God's face and His will for your life. Seeking the Lord now does not mean everything in your life will suddenly become perfect. It does mean God is guarding your path and when you stumble while on this journey, He will be there to catch you.

> *The LORD makes firm the steps of the one who delights in him; though he may stumble, he will not fall, for the LORD upholds him with his hand.* (Psalm 37:23–24, NIV)

As a child, it seemed that Christmas took forever to get here. Now, as an adult, before you can finish paying the credit card bills for last Christmas, the holiday is back again. As we get older, time seems to pass faster and faster. That's why it's so vitally important to guard your time and energy and manage the distractions that come into your life.

Procrastination can kill any good plan. Procrastination must be brought under control and eliminated. You must take some action every day toward implementing your plan and moving toward your goals. Waiting for the perfect time to start your business means you will never start. Waiting for the perfect time to make critical decisions that will grow your business means you will never grow. Waiting for the perfect time to plan means you will never plan (Ecclesiastes 11:4).

PRIORITIES: HOW TO SET THEM

To effectively manage your time is really prioritizing your priorities. That is prioritizing what's important to you. You must set priorities based on the goals you have set. Your goals grow out of the vision God has placed in you. Prioritizing helps to find the work-life balance you need to maintain a steady path to success. With effective time and priority management, you'll spend time working on the important things that move you closer to your goals. You eliminate the things that don't. I have a friend, J.T. Pike, who has a favorite quote he often says: "Don't major in minor." He enjoys conveying the premise that you should not lose sight of the big picture by busying yourself with things that don't really matter. That's good advice. You must spend time on tasks that are important to you and your goals. Also remember that something important to someone else should not automatically become important to you.

This is the point where saying "no" is important. Saying no is difficult for a lot of people. Unless you learn to say no, you can never reach your full potential for success. You are only robbing yourself, your family, and your business of its most valuable resource – you. I suffered from this problem when it came to service on civic and nonprofit boards. At one point in my career, I was on more of these boards than you could shake a stick at. During one year, I was president or chairman of three boards at the same time. As a small-business owner, that was very taxing on time spent in my business. While it's important to give back to the community, there must be limits. I had to learn to say no and I developed a system to effectively manage my time. I set my goals, developed my plan, and prioritized the tasks I needed to perform to move me closer to my goals within the confines of my plan.

For many people, it takes a lot of courage to say no. One of the reasons we tend to say yes to requests that come our way is that most people want to be liked or accepted. We want approval from the people asking us to do things. Here's a news flash. You will never be able to please everyone. So, from the start, have a firm understanding of what your goals are and the things you must do to reach those goals. Having goals and a plan for reaching them gives you confidence to say no. If something is not aligned with your goals and will drain your time, it is OK to politely and firmly decline.

Famed author, Dr. Stephen R. Covey was revolutionary in many ways in his approach to how we should view life, business, personal productivity, principled-centered and spiritual-centered leadership. He encouraged millions around the world. Indeed, the world was saddened and lost a unique visionary with the recent passing of Dr. Covey. Dr. Covey died on July 16, 2012 at the age of 79 in Idaho Falls, Idaho. Dr. Covey developed one of the best time-management systems I have ever seen for achieving goals by identifying every task one can perform and categorizing each task according to importance and urgency. It's amazingly simple but awesomely effective. The process is to place every task in one of four (4)"Quadrants."[88] In Quadrant I, for example, he lists all items that are "Important and Urgent." Items here are <u>important</u> to your goals and must be performed immediately because they are <u>urgent</u> and pressing on you to get done now. Quadrant II contains tasks that are "Important," but "Not Urgent." This is the ideal quadrant to work from because you are able to work on tasks at a comfortable pace. Quadrant III contains items that are "Urgent" but "Not Important." That means these items are not important for your goals, but are items pressing on you which you feel compelled to perform. Quadrant IV items are "Not Important" and "Not Urgent." These are just mindless tasks where you are just wasting time. Being a couch potato for example and watching TV to pass the time.

When setting priorities, do the more difficult tasks first; which means the tasks you are performing should be important to your goals and not meaningless, idle activity. In his book, *"The 21 Most Powerful Minutes in a Leader's Day,"* John Maxwell simply puts it this way: "Activity is not necessarily the accomplishment." By working on the more difficult tasks first, you are removing the more difficult barriers and sources of discouragement that prevent you from achieving your goals and attaining ultimate success. Completing the more difficult tasks first gives you a motivational boost and sense of accomplishment that propels you to finish other tasks that are less difficult.

Many people claim to prioritize, but they often leave out a key ingredient necessary for making prioritizing effective. You must not only prioritize, you must manage the amount of time you spend on the things you have prioritized. Because there are only twenty-four hours in a day and you cannot work during all of them, you must be able to track and measure how much time you are spending on each task. You must allocate more time to the more important tasks and less time on the tasks that are less important. Each day, do the more difficult task first (that's very important). If you finish a task early or ahead of schedule without using all the time you allocated, then you've built up a *reservoir of time* you can dip into that can be used to work on other important tasks that move you toward your goals. I developed my system of time management from years of test taking in law school; which forced me to allocate a limited amount of time to each question or be faced with the prospect of not finishing the exam.

The same is true for accomplishing your goals. You will only be spinning your wheels if you spend productive amounts of your valuable time on meaningless tasks or things that don't move you closer to the goals you set. While you may feel you will live forever and have all the time in the world to get to where you want to go, the reality is your time is limited. Tomorrow is not promised to you. You want to use the time you have wisely and effectively while it is available to you.

POWER POINTS

- Your time on this earth is finite. It's limited. Use it wisely seeking God.
- Procrastination kills good intentions every time.
- The average person has 29,000 days on this earth. Use your time wisely.
- Set priorities. Manage those priorities.
- Spend time working on the important tasks as you have prioritized them.
- Your vision and goals determine what your priorities are.
- Do the hard tasks first, preferably in the mornings.
- Allocate a set amount of time for each task.

Chapter 14

BE A GIVER

A generous person will prosper. Whoever refreshes others will be refreshed.

Proverbs 11:25 (NIV)

SECRET #15: SUCCESSFUL ENTREPRENEURS ARE GIVERS

God's Word is constantly encouraging us to be givers. There is a good reason for that. You simply cannot give to others and not become the recipient of even greater gifts. You can't make others prosperous and not become prosperous yourself, if your motives are good. Sure, man does not have the capacity to create a *perpetual motion machine*, but God does. *That perpetual motion machine* is the act of giving. Yet, so many of us miss the point and miss the blessings that follow from the simple acts of being a giver. Despite God's instruction of the reciprocal benefit of being a giver, we most often turn a deaf ear when it comes to offering to Him our time, talents and resources to feed His sheep. How have you responded to the following verses and how will you respond going forward from here?

- *"Give and it will be given to you. A good measure, pressed down, shaken together and running over, will be poured into your lap. For with the measure you use, it will be measured to you."*[89]
- *"Honor the LORD with your wealth, with the first fruits of all your crops; then your barns will be filled to overflowing, and your vats will brim over with new wine."*[90]
- *"Bring the whole tithe into the storehouse, that there may be food in my house. Test me in this,"* says the LORD Almighty, *"and see if I will not throw open the floodgates of heaven and pour out so much blessing that there will not be room enough to store it."*[91]

If you are not already doing so, you can start by visiting and attending a church and offering your time, talents and resources to that church or its ministries. Don't just "check-the-box" with your attendance or your giving; get involved with making a difference in people's lives. The point here is not that we would give just to get something back. God's concern is for our heart and detaching us from our unhealthy focus on money and material things. In order to get to a place where our relationship with God is right and we are indeed in position to receive, we must have a proper focus on the purpose and benefit of the giving. Matthew 6:19-21 clues us in:

"Do not store up for yourselves treasures on earth, where moths and vermin destroy, and where thieves break in and steal. But store up for yourselves treasures in heaven, where moths and vermin do not destroy, and where thieves do not break in and steal. For where your treasure is, there your heart will be also.'

It's about your salvation and serving others. It's about truly understanding that putting God first means giving to Him the "first fruits" of what we have and earn. So the first priority must be getting the priority correct. That's when the blessings can really flow. The precepts surrounding the concept of "first fruit" and the importance of it is not new and the scriptures are clear about it. Yet it seems foreign to so many. I can personally attest that everything I've ever given has come back to me in more ways than I can ever count, once I truly put God first in my life. Pastor Paula White, in her book, *First Fruit – From Promise to Provision,* puts it in perspective this way:

> *God still considers first things to be holy and devoted to Him, but today first fruits has to do with the practice of keeping the Main Thing, the main thing – and God IS the main thing! First fruits mean the first in place, order and rank; the beginning, chief or principle thing. God says first things belong to Him in order to establish redeeming covenant with everything that comes after. In God's pattern, whatever*

is first establishes the rest. The first is the root, from which the rest is determined. Therefore it is better to destroy your first fruits than to use any of it for your own personal gain.

GIVING IS REALLY RECEIVING

Many blessings are attached to giving. The first and most immediate blessing you will receive from giving is joy. Joy is a powerful gift of strength and encouragement you can and will use in other areas of your life to sustain you, which has nothing to do with the individual or persons you blessed when you gave or reached out to help them.

God is so wise. He prepares our hearts for giving by commanding that we give back to Him first. God knows that unless you can give back to Him first, there is no chance you will have the kind of heart that is willing to give and serve others. When you can give back to God, particularly when financial pressures bear on you or there are demands pressing for your attention, yet you continue to focus on Him, God is preparing you in ways you won't understand. He is preparing you for greater service and to be abundantly blessed. Giving is not necessarily always money. It can be giving of your time, talent, or other resources. But when you give, don't taint the gift by giving it grudgingly. It's best to keep it until whatever is causing you to be so reluctant is removed from your heart. Second Corinthians 9:7 reads: *"Each of you should give what you have decided in your heart to give, not reluctantly or under compulsion, for God loves a cheerful giver."* Why does God require you to be a "cheerful giver?' If the recipient gets the money, what difference does it make? Well, this is why God is so amazing. Being a "cheerful giver" is not about the recipient. It's about you, the giver. It's an overt demonstration that God lives in you and an expression of your love for Him. Moreover, He is preparing you for a life of abundance. That's one of the best kept business secrets in the Bible – God loves a cheerful giver. If that were the case, why aren't more people taking advantage of the time-honored Bible principle?

In today's culture, being a giver goes against the grain. It's not the norm. But the Bible says it is more of a blessing to give than to receive.[92] Indeed, "The Rebekah Principle" as discussed in Chapter 8 under Integrity, gives us the example of why it's so important to have a spirit of giving. By willingly and cheerfully giving above what she was expected to give, Rebekah received a blessing well beyond what I am sure she expected. By going the extra mile in giving, what you receive will by far exceed what you give.

LET YOUR GOODNESS SHOW

Many people, particularly those in business, often think it's not good to be viewed as giving, kind, or compassionate. They prefer to project a persona of being hard-nosed, tough, and having a "take-no-prisoners" attitude. But Romans 12:2 tells us: *"And do not be conformed to this world, but be transformed by the renewing of your mind, that you may prove what is that good and acceptable and perfect will of God."*

The leadership of Jesus Christ transformed the world, and He did it, not by conforming to the ways of the world, but by doing the will of His Father. Being a giver is not the world's way, but it is Christ's way and should be your way. Being a giver emanates from the quality of goodness, which is "*a fruit of the spirit.*"[93] Dr. David Jeremiah describes goodness as "a quality of generosity and openheartedness." When you are a giver and doing good, you are doing God's work. Third John 1:11 (NIV) says: *"Dear friend, do not imitate what is evil but what is good. Anyone who does what is good is from God. Anyone who does what is evil has not seen God."*

Jesus Christ tells us that people will know that we are His followers when we show love for one another. Second Corinthians 8:7 says, *"But since you excel in everything – in faith, in speech, in knowledge, in complete earnestness and in the love we have kindled in you, see that you also excel in this grace of giving."* So it is OK to be a giver and not conform to the world's selfish standard that says it is all about me first.

Often, people don't know how to treat givers. It throws them off. They become discombobulated. Try doing something nice for someone and don't expect anything in return. See what kind of reaction you get. Sometimes they think something is wrong with *you*! It really messes them up – in a good way! When someone observes an act of goodness or kindness taking place, I believe it cultivates the seeds in the observer, which God deposited when He created us in His own image.[94] Thus, His goodness and kindness spreads. So by being a giver, you become the hands of God. What an honor!

On one occasion while shopping in Wal-Mart, I was behind an elderly woman whose check card was rejected after several swipes. People in the line of the crowded store were becoming impatient. The cost of the items was about $50. Among the items I saw were baby diapers, most likely for a grandchild. Before the lady could step aside, I reached into my pocket and handed the cashier enough cash to pay for the items. The cashier appeared stunned and looked around as though she was seeking a manager to approve the transaction. After gathering herself, the cashier said, "Thank you very much," and so did the elderly woman whose eyes were stretched wide in disbelief.

I don't tell that story to toot my own horn. Rather, it illustrates that I received the gift of joy in that moment in being able to give. I could also remember times when I would not have had the ability to give $50, and that thought prompted gratefulness in me for the blessings I now enjoy. Others had certainly helped me along the way many times. When I am traveling and staying at a hotel, as I frequently do, I also find joy in leaving a tip for the maid on top of the Gideon Bible I used for my morning devotion. I thank Gideons International for those Bibles in hotels and the opportunity to share using the Bible when I travel.

I have enjoyed hearing about the many stories of lives being touched by an "Acts of Kindness" initiative our church is promoting through members at the Church of the Highlands. Our senior pastor, Chris Hodges encourages all members to give and show acts of kindness to total strangers by leaving an extra large tip or anonymously paying for someone's meal, but leaving a card for them that says: "*Something Extra to Show That God Loves You.*" It's particularly effective in a fast-food drive-through line. I had a nice chuckle recently, seeing a cashier's face light up when I paid for the order of the car behind me and left a card at a Montgomery Chick-Fil-A. At one fast-food restaurant, I am told this act by a member started a chain reaction and customers paid for the food of other customers behind them for twenty-five cars deep! It's truly a blessing to know that there is so much good in the hearts of God's people. It is also amazing how true God is to His Word when He says, "*give and it will be given to you.*"

FAVOR: GOD'S POWER BOOSTER

In the business world, you don't want to be out there naked. Like the rocket boosters that propelled the Space Shuttle into orbit for so many years, you need the favor of God working to protect and propel you toward your goals. So it was in the familiar story of Joseph. God's favor is all you need to be granted success in all you do. In Genesis 39:2–5 (NIV) we find these words:

> *The LORD was with Joseph so that he prospered, and he lived in the house of his Egyptian master. When his master saw that the LORD was with him and that the LORD gave him success in everything he did, Joseph found favor in his eyes and became his attendant. Potiphar put him in charge of his household, and he entrusted to his care everything*

he owned. From the time he put him in charge of his household and of all that he owned, the LORD blessed the household of the Egyptian because of Joseph. The blessing of the LORD was on everything Potiphar had, both in the house and in the field.

God's favor can open doors no one can close and can close doors no one can open. In Psalms 5:12 we find these words: "*Surely, LORD, you bless the righteous; you surround them with your favor as with a shield.*" What a reassurance that is for us.

Early in my law practice, I needed to take out a bank loan to relocate my office. The sum was more than three times the amount the loan officer had the authority to grant. The loan officer was not very reassuring and said to me, "I will have to take this to the loan committee and talk to the president." The next day the loan officer called me with great excitement, informing me that the loan had been approved. I learned later that the president of the bank, Lester Henderson, knew of some charitable work I had been doing, and I'm sure gave the committee a little nudge. But ultimately, I attribute this approval to the favor of God.

Later, when I met Lester, it was the beginning of a great friendship. He invited me to serve on the board for the American Heart Association, where I was blessed to become one of its presidents. Lester's son, "Les," was my son's baseball coach in high school, and I had an opportunity to work with Lester's wife, Christine, as legal counsel for the school system where she was the caring principal of a school for children with special needs. Christine Henderson also wrote a wonderful book about getting into the will of God after she had a heart attack. The book is entitled, *The Heart of the Matter*, published by New Voice Publishing, LLC.

On the very day I began, in earnest, writing the last chapter of this book on *"Being a Giver,"* Pastor Joel Osteen did a TV broadcast where he preached a sermon entitled "Helping Others Win." The message was about how when we give of ourselves and help others win, that we win too. He talked about how joy abounds when we lift others up.

Tears welled in my eyes when Pastor Osteen told the story of a young special-needs boy named Shay who was allowed to play in a little league baseball game by members of a local team at his father's request. He told how the opposing team allowed Shay, in the last inning, to hit the ball, run the bases as they intentionally overthrew the ball, and allowed him to score the game-winning run.

Hearing that story was memorable for me because, as a little league coach years ago, there were times when the same situation played out with either my team or other teams on the field. Each time, the boys eagerly joined in the opportunity to encourage a special-needs teammate or one on the other team with fewer abilities to safely reach a base or score. Without any urging from coaches, it was as though their hearts spoke to each other and they knew exactly what to do. Their faces all beamed with joy, some jumping, screaming, and even hugging each other in seeing their friend successfully reach the base or score. The excitement they displayed was as if they, themselves, had accomplished the feat. Helping others win creates unthinkable joy.

FAVOR HAS DRAWING POWER

As a young boy, Greg Calhoun, who grew up in one of the poorest sections of Montgomery, Alabama, supported himself by working as a bag boy in a local grocery store. Greg had a wonderful work ethic and dreamed of owning a grocery store one day. Greg's diligence and hard work eventually moved him up the chain to management, where he learned quickly the ins and outs of the grocery business. One day the owner of the store decided he was going to either sell the store or close it. When Greg learned of this, he was able to borrow enough money to purchase the store. The going was rough, but Greg persevered. In order to survive, Greg knew that he needed a relationship with a large food distribution wholesaler. That's when he met Rod Frazer. Rod is a visionary businessman who at the time was the chairman and CEO of Enstar, a large holding company with many global interests. Rod took Greg under his wing and introduced him to the people at Albertson's Foods. As a result of the relationship with Albertson's, Greg was not only able to purchase all the grocery items he needed for one store, he was able to buy several stores, and today he has seventeen stores in the Southeast. Greg has since moved into telecommunications and other business interests. Greg acknowledges that God's favor was upon him when the door was opened to Albertson's through the giving spirit of Rod Frazer.

To put it most simply, when you are a giver, you are planting seeds that will grow and bear fruit for those to whom you give. Equally important is that your gift, whether it be time, money, a smile, or a helping hand will bear fruit for you in the form of favor from God. When you refuse to give, you empty your tank. There is an old adage that says: "A man, by keeping his fist closed tightly keeps riches from getting out, but in so doing, he keeps more from getting in." Pastor Paula White, in her book, *First Fruit,* says: "Withholding will lead to lack in our own lives." Proverbs 11:24–26 puts it this way:

> *One person gives freely, yet gains even more; another withholds unduly, but comes to poverty. A generous person will prosper; whoever refreshes others will be refreshed. People curse the one who hoards grain, but they pray God's blessing on the one who is willing to sell.*

Words cannot express how important it is for you to develop the heart of a giver and actually be a giver. It is a way to separate yourself from the unrelenting influences of the world. It is a key to how you demonstrate your love for your fellowman and show them you are truly a child of God.

In John 34:35 we find the following words of Jesus Christ: *"A new command I give you: Love one another. As I have loved you, so you must love one another. By this everyone will know that you are my disciples, if you love one another."*

FAVOR KEEPS YOU CONNECTED

IIn the very hour I was finishing the first draft of my manuscript and preparing to send it to a friend, Labarron Boone, I received a text message from another friend, Chuck Harris. I had not spoken to Chuck in about three months. Chuck and I often prayed over the phone for each other, our families, and things we were involved in. His text is an example of what we should do when God puts someone on our mind: Reach out, call, or just pray for them. You never know why the person is on your mind, but you should listen to that small voice and be obedient. This is the text Chuck sent me:

"Terry,

A word for today is "Look again." In 2 Kings 6:15–17, Elisha is surrounded by the enemy and asks the Lord to open the eyes of His servant. Given the Lord's touch and a second look the servant could see that there were more with Elisha than with the enemy as he saw the Lord's horses and chariots of fire surrounding Elisha in the mountains. The Lord is with you today, Terry. We can walk in boldness and the authority of his Word even when the view of his rescue isn't immediately clear.

Your Brother,
Chuck Harris"

I thank God for Chuck and the fact that God laid it on his heart to reach out to me. It was exactly what I needed. I was feeling burdened as there appeared a number of challenges that could block me publishing this book and transitioning into a new profession. But Chuck's words and the scripture he cited powerfully uplifted and encouraged me at just the right time. But even more than that, his text demonstrates the power of God's Word and proves God's Word is truly alive. Chuck had no idea when God moved him, that the encouraging words God gave him would not only motivate me, but they would also appear in the pages of this book or that *you* would now be reading the story of Elisha from 2 Kings 6:15–17. In fact, I had not shared with Chuck that I was writing a book. Chuck is an energetic and anointed minister of the Gospel and has had a positive influence on my life for many years. Chuck's text to me also demonstrates the *"connectedness"* and *"relevance"* of God's word to us in today's world. Just as God's favor protected Elisha as a "shield" in a time of trouble, that same favor and protection is available to you and me right now! Also read where David wrote in Psalms 5:12 about God's favor that protects you as a shield. Every day, I claim God's favor and protection on the sometimes treacherous path to business success.

Givers are also servants who plant seeds of goodness, which God calls us to do. Where are you planting seeds of goodness? Be a giver and keep making deposits in your heavenly bank account. God's favor will be upon you and the ROI (Return on Investment) will come back to you faster and more plentiful than you can imagine. As the gospel song goes, *"You can't beat God's giving,"* no matter how hard you try."

POWER POINTS

- Give and it will be given to you.
- Honor the Lord with your wealth and with the first fruit of all your crops.
- Blessings are attached to giving.
- Be joyful in giving. God loves a cheerful giver.
- When you give and do good, you are doing God's work.
- Giving brings you into favor with God.
- God's favor brings prosperity.

Chapter 15

HAVE FAITH IN GOD

Now faith is the substance of things hoped for, the evidence of things not seen.

(Hebrews 11:1)

SECRET #15: SUCCESSFUL ENTREPRENEURS HAVE FAITH IN GOD

Faith is the cornerstone through which you can access all that God provides and reveals to you. It is the vehicle through which you connect to God and allow Him to do wonderful and amazing supernatural things beyond what you can think or imagine. Through faith, God makes things happen for you, including making you a better person in becoming more Christ-like. Once you receive Jesus Christ, into your heart, faith is the single most important personal connection you can have in the battle to find joy and success in starting operating or growing your small business. Your faith puts God firmly in your corner and to work for you in a major way. I say that because our faith pleases God and Hebrews 11:6 specifically says: *And without faith it is impossible to please God, because anyone who comes to him must believe that he exists and that he rewards those who earnestly seek him.* So, how do we please God? Rick Warren, in his book *The Purpose Driven Life* says we please God by offering Him "worship"; being in "relationship" with Him upon being born again; become more "like Jesus Christ"; and give Him your "ministry or service".[95] The result is our faith grows stronger.

Faith is the best <u>defensive</u> weapon you have in protecting your thoughts, plans and actions against the attacks of Satan. ["In addition to all this, take up the shield of faith, with which you can extinguish all the flaming arrows of the evil one." Ephesians 6:16] Faith is not "mere mental assent to a set of religious propositions."[96] Faith is a living, trusting, persevering belief and relationship with God that brings those things in the spiritual realm into the physical realm. As you persevere through the challenges and pressures that come with running a business, you will be tested and called upon to make decisions that will point to your faith. Will you rely on your faith and the Word of God in your decision making process or will you do things totally your way? The hope is that you will turn to God's Word, where your character will be strengthened and your faith will increase as you allow God to guide you through the minefields or the business battlefield. Through the exercise of your faith, you will gain valuable insight into how to run and grow your business.

If I had to give a literal example of how faith works, I'd say Proverbs 3:5-6 (NJKV) nails it! (no pun intended) *"Trust in the Lord with all your heart, lean not to your own understanding. In all your ways acknowledge Him and He shall direct your path."* It is by faith that we let go of our own feeble efforts to deal with challenges and rely on revelations of God through the Holy Spirit to guide direct our actions and reactions to the circumstances of life. In Chapter 6, I pointed to 1 Corinthians 2:10–12, which tells us exactly how the Holy Spirit works to reveal God's truths that He wants us to know which in turn increases our faith:

> *These are the things God has revealed to us by his Spirit. The Spirit searches all things, even the deep things of God. For who knows a person's thoughts except their own spirit within them? In the same way no one knows the thoughts of God except the Spirit of God. What we have received is not the spirit of the world, but the Spirit who is from God, so that we may understand what God has freely given us.*

As an entrepreneur operating in the marketplace, your faith will be tested in many different circumstances. In a conversation about faith I had with Meredith Jackson, a friend and pastor, he told me a story about two farmers that was revealing about the levels of one's faith. One farmer, he said, prayed to God for rain, watched the sky and waited. The other farmer, after praying, went out and plowed his fields. So which farmer would you say exercised the greater level of faith? Who was better prepared to receive God's blessing when it came?

Whenever the occasion arose for the Apostle Paul to exercise faith in the presence of others, he became excited and highly motivated because he knew the Gospel of Jesus Christ would spread. When you exercise your faith and witness to another what God has done for you, you have removed yourself from being a "spectator Christian" into the realm of "active participant" in spreading the Gospel. In Romans 1:16-17, this is what Paul says about the power of what the Gospel does for each of us and how the righteousness of God is revealed by faith:

> *For I am not ashamed of the Gospel of Christ, for it is the power of God to salvation for everyone who believes, for the Jew first and also for the Greek. For in it the righteousness of God is revealed from faith to faith; as it is written, The just shall live by faith.*

FAITH AND FINANCE

Some say you cannot strive to amass financial wealth and still maintain a strong faith in Jesus Christ. I have not seen that in the Bible. What I have seen is this: In Matthew 6:24 (NIV), it reads:

> *No one can serve two masters. Either you will hate the one and love the other, or you will be devoted to the one and despise the other. You cannot serve both God and money.*

This scripture does not say you should not seek to acquire financial wealth. But it does mean that the money you acquire should not become your "god." But for all too many, their only comfort and sense of worth is in the size of their bank account. That is a dangerous place to be and God's Word speaks to this. Contrary to popular belief, the Bible does not say "money is the root of all evil." This is why knowing God's Word for yourself is so important. The scripture actually says it is the *love* of money that is evil.

> *For the love of money is a root of all kinds of evil, for which some have strayed from the faith in their greediness, and pierced themselves through with many sorrows.*
>
> 1 Timothy 6:10

Money or the lack of it will constantly test your faith and your relationship with God. To maintain the correct focus, you should frequently ask yourself these three questions: 1) What am I doing on a consistent basis to grow closer to Jesus Christ? 2) What good am I doing in the world? And, 3) Am I giving back to God at least ten (10%) percent of that with which He has entrusted to me? Joshua set the standard for obedience to God's commands when he said, "*As for me and my house, we will follow the Lord*" (Joshua 24:15). I love that sense of spiritual conviction. No matter what other people decide to do or not do, Joshua stepped up and declared his active faith in God, which is exactly the place where each of us should strive to be.

It's very easy in the business world to only be concerned about the bottom line. Such a narrow focus can cause you to lose out on something even more important, your salvation. A great story is told in Luke 18:18–23 about a rich young ruler who asks Jesus what he must do to inherit eternal life:

> *A certain ruler asked him, "Good teacher, what must I do to inherit eternal life?" "Why do you call me good?" Jesus answered. "No one is good – except God alone. You know the commandments: You shall not commit adultery, you shall not murder, you shall not steal, you shall not give false testimony, honor your father and mother." "All these I have kept since I was a boy," he said.*
>
> *When Jesus heard this, he said to him, "You still lack one thing. Sell everything you have and give to the poor, and you will have treasure in heaven. Then come, follow me."*
>
> *When he heard this, he became very sad, because he was very wealthy. Jesus looked at him and said, "How hard it is for the rich to enter the kingdom of God! Indeed, it is easier for a camel to go through the eye of a needle than for someone who is rich to enter the kingdom of God."*

Business people sometimes read this passage and worry. Does God actually want everybody to sell everything? The simple answer is, it depends. The point is that money was an obstacle between this man and his salvation. If money was the obstacle, then the obstacle needed to be eradicated. Jesus instructed the young ruler [as he instructs each of us] you can't take it with you. However, by giving it to the poor, you can send it ahead!

The fact is God wants to abundantly bless and prosper you. He wants to give you as much influence and wealth as you desire because He knows that you are called to use that wealth and influence to do His good works. In the process many will see His work in you, they will grow in faith and find salvation. As an entrepreneur who has faith, God's words in Deuteronomy 28:8 should fill you with excitement and expectation where He says:

> *The LORD will command the blessing on you in your storehouses and in all to which you set your hand, and He will bless you in the land which the LORD your God is giving you.*

Whether you have "money" or not, it is your faith that keeps you grounded. So, what is faith? The Bible tells us that *"faith is the substance of things hoped for, the evidence of things not seen."*[97] Before setting goals and establishing plans for your business, study and expose yourself to God's Word, so that you will learn how your faith can be strengthened. Romans 10:17 says: *"So then faith comes by hearing, and hearing by the Word of God."*

Faith is the source that gives you the confidence to know you can reach the goals you establish and fulfill those plans to develop your business. My pastor, Chris Hodges put it this way in one of his recent sermons: *"Some say they can never experience God until they understand, but I say they can never understand until they experience God."* Put another way, *"faith is not seeing it to believe it, faith is believing it to see it."* Through faith, you know that God loves you so much that He sent His only Son that you and I would have life everlasting.[98] Through faith, you learn that God prepares and equips you for the work ahead you must do. Second Timothy 3:16–17 says: *"All Scripture is God-breathed and is useful for teaching, rebuking, correcting and training in righteousness, so that the servant of God may be thoroughly equipped for every good work."*

Through faith, God will reveal the right choices to you, even when you feel your choices may be limited. Consider the plight of Joseph as found in Matthew 1:18–20:

> *This is how the birth of Jesus the Messiah came about: His mother Mary was pledged to be married to Joseph, but before they came together, she was found to be pregnant through the Holy Spirit. Because Joseph her husband was faithful to the law, and yet did not want to expose her to public disgrace, he had in mind to divorce her quietly.*
>
> *But after he had considered this, an angel of the Lord appeared to him in a dream and said, "Joseph, son of David, do not be afraid to take Mary home as your wife, because what is conceived in her is from the Holy Spirit."*

Here was Joseph, a man whose wife had been pledged to him, but he learned that his wife was with child, and it wasn't his child. It was known that Joseph was a decent man who followed the law. As a result, Joseph felt he only had two choices: 1) Expose her to public disgrace, where she would be stoned to death; or 2) divorce her quietly. But an angel of God came to Joseph and gave him a third option, which was to marry her! That's right – marry her! If this had happened in today's culture, I can imagine that Joseph's response would have been something like: "Come on Man!" Or, "You can't be serious!" or, "Yeah, right!" I'm thankful this didn't happen in today's culture. But think about the strength, courage, fortitude, and faith it took for Joseph to be obedient to God's Word with so many looking on. It was faith and obedience that led Joseph to the correct decision. The scripture tells us in Mathew 17:20 that the *"faith of a mustard seed can move mountains."* What we do know is that Joseph had to be under a great deal of pressure in the culture of that day. In his hands he had the power of life and death. Joseph's decision had implications far beyond anything he could have imagined. We, as Christians can all be thankful for the faith and obedience that Joseph exhibited. As we can now attest, Joseph made the right decision despite his personal circumstance, potential public humiliation and pressure. Because he made the right choice, humanity was given a second chance. Praise be to God!

God tells us He will never leave us or forsake us.[99] If you believe and trust in Him, His favor will be upon you, and success and victory is yours to claim. You will find His favor will open many doors. It is through faith you can count your blessings and thank God everyday for them. Through faith, you can thank him for the opportunities you have before you right now. You can thank Him for the good health you have now or the healing you will experience in the days to come. You are able to thank Him for a sound mind, strength and joy you've experienced. It is through faith that you are able to thank him for the journey over which He has brought you.

There will be times in your life when burdens will wear you down. Often the burdens have nothing to do directly with the business, but you nevertheless must deal with them. It is your faith, in these times, that provides the strength from within to enable you to persevere. That strength comes from God's mighty power within you.[100]

That's the real purpose of this book – to help prepare you with an inner guidance system that you can only *receive* from the Gospel of Jesus Christ and Bible teachings. This guidance system, on which your faith is built, will navigate you through the rough and smooth waters of starting, operating, and growing a business. It is through your faith that you will *achieve* great things as you find strength, prosperity, and peace on the journey.

FAITH IS A COMPASS

Like Noah, in many situations, your faith is all you will have to direct and guide you. In Hebrews 11:7 we find these words: *"By faith Noah, being divinely warned of things not yet seen, moved with godly fear, prepared an ark for the saving of his household, by which he condemned the world and became heir of the righteousness which is according to faith."* Even in the midst of what may seem like insurmountable obstacles, you will find strength and incredible peace on this journey.[101] It is through your faith that you will gain confidence and courage. Faith is what pulls it all together and prepares you for the journey. It was faith that led Chick-Fil-A's founder, S. Truett Cathy, to close all his stores on Sundays so he and his employees could attend church. A Sunday-School teacher, Cathy asked one teenage boy, "What would you think if you knew that my cash registers were jingling while I was teaching this lesson on the observance of the Lord's Day? The boy answered, "I would think you are a hypocrite."[102] Chick-Fil-A is one of the country's most successful restaurants and Cathy will tell you, "We generate more sales in our restaurants in six days than many other chains do in seven."[103]

With faith, you will gain knowledge, wisdom, and an understanding of how to succeed. Your faith will show you the power of speaking blessings upon yourself. Don't be like so many others who constantly tell themselves they are not smart enough or don't have the talent or ability to excel at something challenging. There are enough negative forces and people already out there that are ready to put you down and shake your confidence and your faith. So why should you help them? That's what is not smart. Your faith and connection to God will tell you to speak only of the abundance and blessings that have been promised to you. Your faith will tell you whether or not this business is a stepping stone to prepare you for greater success. Even where one door is closed, another door will be opened.

God is a refuge for *whatever* circumstance comes your way.[104] But you will never know that until you try Him by exercising faith.

The darts of depression, discouragement, and doubt can cause you to do strange things and make choices you thought you would never make. These darts can cause you to do harm not only to yourself, but to others, including those you love. By having faith in God, meditating on His Word, and exercising your faith, you will be empowered to overcome and defeat these darts. By faith, you know and understand that you are under the protection of the blood of Jesus Christ and guided by the Holy Spirit. In God's Word you will know that there is *no circumstance, no circumstance, no circumstance* too big for God to handle. Anytime doubt or fear approach you, immediately call to mind the words Jesus spoke to Peter in Matthew 16:18, "*On this rock I will build my church and the gates of hell shall not prevail against it.*" In Jesus Christ, you cannot be defeated by the things Satan places before you. On this journey to success we never speak of failure. It is not an option. We only speak of opportunities to learn and exercise our faith in God as we move closer to Christ and press on to the mark of the goals we have set. The battle has already been won and God's purposes will be served no matter the circumstance we face or what we have to endure. [105] You have the shield of faith to protect you and Word of God as your sword.[106] Always remain confident in the knowledge that it is through faith and prayer that we allow God's mighty power to bestow upon us the abundant blessings and success He has promised us!

POWER POINTS

- Faith is the substance of things hoped for, the evidence of things not seen.
- Faith is the cornerstone by which we access everything God provides us.
- Faith is not mere mental assent to a set of religious propositions.
- Faith is a living, trusting persevering belief and relationship with God.
- Do not let money or material things become your god.
- Give 10 percent or more or your income back to God.
- Exercise faith, particularly when your finances are tight.
- Faith is your bridge and compass for getting into God's will.
- Always speak blessings on yourself. Words have power.
- By faith we understand there is *no circumstance* too big for God.
- Faith works through the Holy Spirit.
- The just shall live by faith.
- The LORD will command the blessing on you in your storehouses and in all to which you set your hand.

###

About QR Codes

http://receiveandachievenow.com/aboutqr

Those little black squares are popping up everywhere. But what are they? Each one is called a "QR Code" (abbreviated from Quick Response Code). The QR Code was invented in Japan by the Toyota subsidiary, Denso Wave, in 1994 to track vehicles during the manufacturing process. QR Codes have in recent years become common in consumer advertising and packaging, because the dissemination of Smartphone's "has put a barcode reader in everyone's pocket for the first time." The same is true for tablet computers equipped with cameras. As a result, the QR code has become a focus of advertising strategy, since it provides quick and effortless access to a sponsor's website or videos.[107] Creating QR codes and obtaining apps for QR readers is for the most part free.

However, if you want tracking or develop a marketing campaign, these services can be obtained for a fee.

We are using QR Codes (and traditional links) in *Receive and Achieve Now!* to enhance your reading and learning experience and to give you quick robust access to my website, scripture references, blogs, videos, audio files my coaching program and even webinars or teleseminars. The objective is to put the reading and learning experience of print versions of this book on par with ebook readers, tablet computers, the iPad, iPhone, Kindle, the Nook and other ebook readers in terms of immediate access to information.

We are excited about this rapidly emerging technology and pleased to be among the first in the world to offer these features it in both printed and digital/e-book versions of the book using *IMFAX Smartbook Technology*™ to do so.

My team was concerned that not enough was being published about how QR codes work and what downsides may exist. So, we interviewed A. R. Austin, is a CISSP and ITIL certified Internet security engineer who supports the *IMFAX Smartbook Technology*™ resource tool to help educate our readers. He provided the following information and four (4) important tips to remember about QR codes:

Mr. Austin:

> "QR Codes are very useful, practical and efficient tools designed for interactive use in commerce. They can perform a variety of functions. The most commonly known use, outside industrial markets, is

quick access, via a smartphone to a website, landing page or targeted online information to educate a reader or convert the user to become a customer. The use of QR codes in this manner is effective because typically a prospect will only scan a QR code if that person has a particular interest in the subject matter, product or service being displayed by the company or person who generated the QR code. The same functions can be accomplished through other mediums, but businesses are beginning to develop complete marketing campaigns, training and education platforms using QR codes because of their ease of use. Scanning activity can be tracked and metrics or reports provided on that activity, including location of the scan. But like any technology using the Internet, QR codes can be used to take your smartphone to a malicious website or embed a virus on it, so caution should be exercised. Because the prevalence of QR codes will increase drastically in the coming months and years, here are some tips to put you ahead of the game:

*1. **Be certain the QR code you scan is safe**. Look at the source that is offering the QR code. Is it from a company with brand-name products or from a reliable source with whom you are familiar with? Several major corporations are including QR codes in their* sales and marketing strategies. National companies like H.H. Gregg, Walgreens and Wal-Mart have all begun using QR codes in their advertising fliers. McDonalds, for example, is accelerating its use of QR codes and will likely be embedding its color logo into the black and white code so it is visible and will further promote its brand. Even though most QR codes today are black and white, some QR codes will be multiple colors. QR codes that are invisible to the naked eye are also being introduced. As another example, this book, is a safe source because the QR codes and websites have been produced by a known source. Every company using this technology should be offered a higher level of education about it because attacks on mobile devices are on the increase.

2. **Get a QR code app that will check the website before allowing it to be downloaded on your Smartphone**. The app works just like anti-virus software and will block malicious sites or suspect files that may be infected with a virus from your smartphone. Some can also preview a site and alert you as to whether it's safe to proceed. Symantec and McAfee are leading companies that can provide and recommend to you free apps and resources to protect your smart phone. They also sell software

and services that can protect your device and data. You need that protection because the bad guys even have the ability to redirect your smart phone to an infected site.

3. **Never provide personal information such as social security numbers, driver's license numbers, passwords or date of birth to a suspect QR Code scanned site**. Such requests are always a recipe for disaster. Leave any site immediately that requests such personal information.

4. **Be vigilant and use good judgment regarding offers at scanned sites that sound too good to be true**. Never provide credit card or banking information to a site unless you are able to independently verify the site or source requesting the info is legitimate."

Use of this technology is providing a little glimpse into the future. It will be used in many ways in the coming months. I am thankful to God that we are on this journey together and have a bird's eye view. In Chapter 6, I spoke about "Spotting the Waves of Change." Your awareness now and use of this technology is an example of how visionaries and successful entrepreneurs spot and get in front of the waves of change which they ultimately act on and benefit from. This book represents the tip of the iceberg of the myriad of uses for QR code technology. But you are witnessing an evolution of how, in the near future, we will learn, access, receive and retrieve information and knowledge. QR codes are already seeping into our everyday culture. Check the sales pages in your newspaper. Look around. Some stores already offer discounts for scanning QR codes about their products. Examine magazines, cups at fast-food places and newspapers such as *USA Today*. When watching a commercial on TV, you will soon be able to scan a QR code that is displayed for a product during a commercial and use it as a coupon or to learn more about the product.

Don't let any of this overwhelm you because God is still on His Throne and in charge. This technology is an example of how God allows individuals to use the gift of to "*call those things which do not exist as though they did*" to create and manifest great things. God has promised us that he has more abundance in store for us than we can "*think or imagine.*" It's up to each of us to get into His perfect will to? claim it. We must however remain vigilant in our use of any technology. Don't forget Mr. Austin's advice and obtain a free app to protect your smartphone when you scan a QR code.

ABOUT THE AUTHORS

TERRY G. DAVIS, JD, MBA

Terry G. Davis is an author, attorney, entrepreneur, negotiation consultant and executive business coach. He is the founder of SmartBizUniversity.com™. Terry has served as counsel and chief strategist for several successful start-ups, including the company that was the first to introduce global Internet service to the commercial cruise-line industry, a service currently in use in the U.S. and Europe.

Terry received a bachelor's degree from Alabama State University, an MBA from Auburn University Montgomery and a Doctorate of Jurisprudence from Cumberland School of Law at Samford University. In 2009, Terry was named one of Auburn University Montgomery's Top 40 Graduates. Terry is married and has two children. He is an active member of Church of the Highlands, Montgomery, Alabama.

REV. DAVID L. MORROW

David L. Morrow is a graduate of the University of North Carolina at Chapel Hill, where he earned a degree in psychology in 1976. After graduating from Southeastern Theological Seminary, Wake Forest, North Carolina, with a Master of Divinity degree in 1983, he was commissioned for active-duty service and served in the United States Air Force Chaplain Corps for twenty-seven years. While serving active duty, he received a Master of Arts in Christian Education from the Presbyterian School of Christian Education, Richmond, Virginia, and a Master of Strategic Studies from the Air War College, Air University, Maxwell Air Force Base, Montgomery, Alabama. David retired as a Colonel and currently resides in Durham, North Carolina. He is married and has two children.

End Notes

1. Unless otherwise indicated, version is King James Version.
2. Matthew 28:19 (NIV); 1 Peter 2:9(NIV).
3. Proverbs 18:16 (NIV).
4. James 3:17 (NIV).
5. 1 Peter 5:8 (NKJV).
6. Isaiah 14:12-13 (NKJV).
7. Infra
8. Chris Hodges, David Jeremiah, John Maxwell, T.D. Jakes, Charles Stanley, Joel Osteen, Paula White, Joyce Meyer, Jesse Duplantis, Michael Dell, Steve Ballmer, John Thompson, Carly Fiorina, A.G. Gaston, Scott McNealy, David L. Steward, Rob Tarkoff, Sr. Michael Jones, Robert Lynch, Douglas McMillon, Marvin Carroll, William Pickard, George Fraser, Fabienne Fredrickson, Karl Bryan, Michael Phillips, Warren Buffett, Greg Calhoun, Michael Roberts, Dave Ramsey, Eben Pagan, Tony Robbins, Brendon Burchard, Brian Tracy, John Eggen, Napoleon Hill, Dennis Kimbro, Joe L. Reed, Robert Allen, Lisa Nichols. Listing of these personalities is not an indication of an endorsement of this book.
9. Ecclesiastes 12:13.
10. Chart originated from Duane Donner, CEO, Founders Investment Banking, LLC, 2204 Lakeshore Drive, Suite, 425, Birmingham, AL 35209.
11. Ecclesiastes 12:13, Secrets of the Vine, Bruce Wilkerson, (p 105)
12. 12 John 14:15
13. Psalm 121:1–3.
14. Ephesians 6:18.
15. Battlefield of the Mind, Joyce Meyer, p.20.
16. John 16:23-24.
17. Psalm 37:5.

18. Eben Pagan, www.gurumasterclass.com
19. Dennis Kimbro and Napoleon Hill, *Think and Grow Rich: A Black Choice*.
20. http://en.wikipedia.org/wiki/Paul_the_Apostle
21. Luke 18:27 (NIV).
22. Mark Twain.
23. Service now operates under the name of Seamobile. URL www.digitalseas.com redirects to Seamobile.
24. The 21 Most Powerful Minutes in a Leader's Day, John Maxwell.
25. Psalms 37:5.
26. Ephesians 1:18-20.
27. Philippians 4:6 (NIV).
28. Proverbs 4:5-6 (NIV).
29. Malachi 3:10.
30. Exodus 3:1–4:17, and God's call of David, 1 Samuel 16:1–13.
31. Ephesians 3:20.
32. Mark 4:20.
33. 2 Chronicles 1:7-12.
34. Nehemiah 6:15.
35. See http://www.smart-goals.org/.
36. http://en.wikipedia.org/wiki/SWOT_analysis.
37. Mission Marketing Mentors, Inc. calls it a "Task and Mire Checklist in book publishing."
38. Dr. Charles Stanley, sermon entitled *"Facing Obstacles."*
39. Ephesians 6:16
40. Luke 4:1-13
41. Ask Jeeves.com.
42. Hebrews 12:7–11 (NIV).
43. Revelation 12:10-12
44. John 3:16.
45. Ephesians 6:16.
46. Philippians 3:14 (NKJV).
47. http://en.wikipedia.org/wiki/Cadillac_Williams; http://bleacherreport.com/articles/648076-the-ten-best-running-backs-in-auburn-history/page/10.
48. *The God in You*, David Jeremiah.
49. Luke 24:32 (NIV).
50. http://en.wikipedia.org/wiki/Kelvin_Davis_(basketball)
51. James 2:26 (NIV).
52. *Good Guys Finish First*, Clinton W. McLemore.
53. (*Action Has No Season*, © 2008 Michael V. Roberts).

54 (*The Knowledge Link*, © 1991, Joseph L. Badaracco Jr, Harvard Business School Press, p. 48).
55 http://www.anselm.edu/homepage/dbanach/h-carnegie-steel.htm.
56 Quoted from John Maxwell's "The 21 Most Powerful Minutes in a Leader's Day.
57 http://www.encyclopedia.com/doc/1O12-wordofmouse.html.
58 Ephesians 2:18.
59 "Leader's bias" is a term taken from John Maxwell's "The 21 Most Powerful Minutes in a Leader's Day."
60 Proverbs 15:22 (NIV).
61 2 Timothy 2:15 (NIV).
62 Proverbs 4:4–9 (NIV).
63 2 Chronicles 10–12(NIV).
64 California, Michigan, Maryland, New Jersey, Delaware and Illinois.
65 Galatians 6:7–9 (NIV).
66 *More Is Caught Than Taught,* Copyright © 1998 by Federation of Child Care Centers of Alabama).
67 http://articles.orlandosentinel.com/1996-11-11/sports/9611100429_1_evander-holyfield-mike-tyson-las-vegas.
68 http://en.wikipedia.org/wiki/Tim_Tebow.
6   Florida QB Tebow was the first underclassman to win the Heisman". ESPN. 2007-12-08. http://sports.espn.go.com/ncf/news/story?id=3146714.
70 http://en.wikipedia.org/wiki/John_W._Thompson
71 "25 Most Influential Evangelicals in America". *TIME*. 2005-02-07. http://www.time.com/time/covers/1101050207/photoessay/18.html.
72 http://www.joycemeyer.org/
73 Deuteronomy 31:6 (NIV).
74 Romans 8:31.
75 Unknown author.
76 1 John 2:12.
77 Matthew 11:28-30.
78 New word.
79 Eat to Live, (Little, Brown and Company, Revised 2011).
80 http://www.apnorc.org/news-media/Pages/News+Media/poll-few-americans-know-all-the-risks-of-obesity.aspx
81 http://www.theheart.org/article/1176761.do.
82 Exodus 20:12 (NIV).
83 Philippians 4:7(NIV).

84	Jeremiah 32:17.
85	Proverbs 3:5.
86	Philippians 4:13 (NKJV).
87	Daniel 3:28-29
88	First Things First, Stephen R. Covey, A. Roger Merrill and Rebecca R. Merrill.
89	Luke 6:38 (NIV).
90	Proverbs 3:8–9.
91	Malachi 3:10 (NIV).
92	Acts 20:35 (NIV).
93	Galatians 5:22.
94	Genesis 1:27 (NIV).
95	The Purpose Driven Life, pp. 64, 118, 171, 228, Rick Warren
96	Bible Expositor and Illuminator, Fall 2012, p. 5, Union Gospel Press Division.
97	Hebrews 11:1(NKJV).
98	John 3:16.
99	Deuteronomy 31:6 (NIV).
100	Ephesians 6:10.
101	Philippians 4:7.
102	How Did You Do It Truett, S. Truett Cathy.
103	Ibid.
104	Psalm 46.
105	Romans 8:28.
106	Ephesians 6:17.
107	http://en.wikipedia.org/wiki/QR_code.